COME BEFORE WINTER

BOOKS BY CYRIL J. BARBER

Successful Church Libraries, with E. Towns
The Minister's Library, 2 vols.
The Minister's Library, vol. 3, with M. L. Bickley
God Has the Answer
Searching for Identity
Nehemiah and the Dynamics of Effective Leadership
Always a Winner, with J. Carter
Vital Encounter
Marriage Enrichment in the Church
Leadership: The Dynamics of Success, with G. Strauss
Introduction to Theological Research
Your Marriage Has Real Possibilities
Ruth: A Story of God's Grace
You Can Have a Happy Marriage
Habakkuk and Zephaniah
Through the Valley of Tears
Your Marriage Can Last a Lifetime
Judges: A Narrative of God's Power
The Books of Samuel, 2 vols.
Best Books for Your Home Bible Study Library
Introduction to Theological Research, rev. ed., with R. Krauss, Jr.
Unlocking the Scriptures
Faithfulness of God, 2 vols.
The Books of Kings, 2 vols.
The Dynamics of Effective Leadership
The Books of Chronicles, 2 vols.
Lord, Please Help Me, My Teenager Is Driving Me Crazy, with G. Strauss.
Joshua: We Will Serve the Lord
Ezra and Esther

Contributor, *Zondervan Pictorial Encyclopedia of the Bible*
Contributor, *New Unger's Bible Dictionary*
Contributor, *Baker's Encyclopedia of the Bible*

COME BEFORE WINTER

PROFILES OF SOME OF PAUL'S FRIENDS

... and some who were not.

by

CYRIL J. BARBER

WIPF & STOCK · Eugene, Oregon

Wipf and Stock Publishers
199 W 8th Ave, Suite 3
Eugene, OR 97401

Come Before Winter
Profiles of Some of Paul's Friends...and some who were not.
By Barber, Cyril J.
Copyright©2008 by Barber, Cyril J.
ISBN 13: 978-1-60608-179-2
Publication date 9/10/2008

(c) Copyright by Cyril J. Barber.

Quotations of Scripture used in this book are from the
New American Standard Bible (NASB),
copyrighted 1960, 1962, 1963, 1971, 1972, 1973, 1975,
1977, 1995
by the Lockman Foundation, and are
used by permission of the Lockman Foundation.

Quotations from the *Holy Bible, New International
Version* (NIV),
copyrighted 1973, 1978, 1984,
by the International Bible Society,
are used by permission of Zondervan Bible Publishers.

Other quotations and/or paraphrases of Scripture
are the author's.

Biblical references in parentheses (e.g., 1:1)
are to the book of Acts.

For . . .

Jim Rosscup

and

In Memory of Mildred Rosscup

and

Bob and Marjorie Williams,

the best of friends for more than forty-five years.

THE AUTHOR

Cyril J. Barber, D. Litt., D.Min., D.D., is the pastor emeritus of Plymouth Church, Whittier, California. He makes his home in Hacienda Heights with Aldyth, his wife of fifty years.

CONTENTS

INTRODUCTION

1. GOD'S MAN IN DAMASCUS — 9
2. THE MAN WHO WAS MISTAKEN FOR A GOD — 23
3. THE POWER OF ENCOURAGEMENT — 37
4. THE SECOND STRING — 53
5. LUKE, PAUL'S BELOVED FRIEND — 63
6. LYDIA — 73
7. SONGS IN THE NIGHT — 81
8. THE HAND OF THE LORD — 93
9. FELIX, THE UNHAPPY GOVERNOR — 105
10. PAUL'S APPEAL TO CAESAR — 117
11. THE VOYAGE TO ROME — 129
12. PAUL'S SUCCESSOR — 143

INTRODUCTION

As I look back on the times I have studied the book of Acts it seems as if each person teaching the class had taken his cue from Joe Friday of *Dragnet*. Sargent Friday and his sidekick would be sent out to investigate a problem. Friday's method of questioning was limited to "Just the facts, Ma'am." As I reflect on these experiences it seems as if my instructors took the same approach and limited their instruction to "just the facts." The result? A boring rehearsal of the data that deprived Luke's account of the vitality that is its due.

Then, after many years, it became my turn to teach this portion of God's Word. I prefer to think of the contents of Luke's book as an illustration of William George Tarrant's[1] poem:

> Now praise we great and famous men,
> The fathers, named in story;
> And praise the Lord, who now as then
> Reveals in man His glory.
> Praise we the wise and brave and strong

---

1. 1853-1928.

Who graced their generation;
Who helped the right, and fought the wrong,
And made our folk a nation.

Praise we the great of heart and mind,
The singers sweetly gifted,
Whose music like a mighty wind
The souls of men uplifted. . . .

We praise the glorious names we know,
And they whose names have perished–
Lost in the haze of long ago–
In silent love be cherished. . . .

So praise we great and famous men,
The fathers, named in story;
And praise the Lord, who now as then
Reveals in man His glory.

No man in the New Testament, apart from the Lord Jesus Himself, is better known than the Apostle Paul. No man had better friends, and no man made fiercer enemies. To some of his friends he sent greetings at the end of his letters. They cluster around him so thickly that we are apt to overlook the part they played in the furtherance of the gospel. The late Dr. Alexander Whyte remarked truthfully of Paul's friends that it is only with the utmost difficulty we get a glimpse of them.

In this book of simple devotional studies I have tried to lift these individuals out of the shadows and, by attempting to recreate the milieu of the first century A.D., describe how they helped the great Apostle to the Gentiles. I have not dealt with all of those with whom the Apostle Paul was acquainted, and those mentioned in his letters will have to wait for a later volume. I trust, however, that what I have written will be a blessing to those who study these pages.

Quotations from the Book of Acts are cited in parentheses, e.g., (16:1).

I am once again indebted my good friends, David Cahn and Maurice Bickley for their help in preparing the manuscript for publication. I can never thank them enough for the assistance they have given me! May the Lord amply reward them!!

CHAPTER ONE

GOD'S MAN IN DAMASCUS

If you were asked to write down the names of those people who had been most influential in your life, who would you list? Mother? Father? Grandparent? Sunday school teacher? Close friend? In the case of the Apostle Paul he could have listed Gamaliel, the eminent doctor of the law, under whom he had studied in Jerusalem; or Caiaphas, the high priest, whom he wanted to impress and so persecuted the early church; or one of the Maccabees? However, as John Knox, the great Scottish reformer, once remarked, "When I think of those who have influenced my life the most, I think not of the great but of the good."[2]

Our influence upon others can be either positive or negative.[3] We don't often think about it, but everywhere we go–at work, in a restaurant, on the phone — we leave some kind of mark. Paul's friends were not numbered among the great, but they were good.[4] Numerous books have been devoted to the life and labors of Paul, but those associated

---

2. This was certainly true of Paul (cf. Romans 16:1-16; 1 Corinthians 16:15-20; Colossians 4:7-15; 2 Timothy 4:19-22; Titus 3:12-15; Philemon 1:23-24).
3. John Dryden in *Alexander's Feast* (I:169) spoke of one's positive encouragement of another as "raising a mortal to the skies." On the other hand, the Apostle Paul likened the negative influence of a person to leaven that "leavens the whole lump" (1 Corinthians 5:6; Galatians 5:9).

with him have been obscured by the mists of time so that they are easily overlooked.

We are inclined to think of Paul as a kind of maverick, but his nature was much like our own. He needed his friends. For example, having sent Timothy back to Thessalonica, Paul arrived in Corinth alone. Later, when he wrote to the Corinthians, he admitted "*I was with you in weakness and in fear and in much trembling*" (1 Corinthians 2:3). A few quotations from his letters further illustrate this point and show how much his associates influenced his life: "I *rejoice* over the coming of Stephanas and Fortunatus and Achaicus ... for *they have refreshed my spirit* ..." (1 Corinthians 16:17-18). Later on he wrote, "when I came to Troas for the gospel of Christ, and when a door was opened for me in the Lord, *I had no rest for my spirit*, not finding Titus my brother; but taking my leave of them, I went on to Macedonia" to look for him (2 Corinthians 2:12-13). A happy encounter followed for which Paul gave thanks: "But God, who comforts the *depressed*, comforted us by the coming of Titus ..." (2 Corinthians 7:6. See also 1 Thessalonians 3:1-2).

The words in italics show us the human side of Paul's nature. He was a man of like passions, and he needed to

---

4. In the early chapters of the book of Acts Paul is referred to as Saul. Saul was his Jewish name. He had been born in Tarsus (22:3), a Roman city, and enjoyed dual citizenship—Jewish and Roman. After 13:9 he is referred to by his Roman name, Paul.

have his friends close at hand to encourage him in his work for the Lord (2 Corinthians 2:12-13).

As we consider the events described in Acts 9 we note that the story of Paul's conversion is divided into two parts: Part I, "A Man on a Murderous Mission" (9:1-9), and Part II, "A Man With a Special Commission" (9:10-19*a*).

A Man On A Murderous Mission

When first we meet Saul/Paul he is on a murderous mission (9:1-2).[5] So fanatical was he that Dr. J. A. Alexander suggested the words "breathing out murderous threats" convey the idea of a ravenous beast devouring a carcass.[6] On the day Stephen was martyred (7:58; 8:1*a*) "a great persecution began against the church in Jerusalem" (8:1*b*). This caused the believers to flee to other towns and villages (8:4). Saul, not satisfied with his attempts to crush the fledgling church in Jerusalem, determined to eradicate followers of Christ in other centers as well. To carry out his purge he decided to go to Syria. In order for his plan to succeed he approached the high priest for "extradition papers" to the leaders of the synagogues in Damascus. These papers gave him authority to bring any who were followers of "The Way" (i.e., believers in Jesus Christ) bound to Jerusalem for scourging, imprisonment and possible execution.

---

5. See Acts 9:1-18; 22:1-12.
6. J. A. Alexander, *Commentary on the Acts of the Apostles*, 2 vols. in 1 (Minneapolis: Klock and Klock, 1980), I:355.

Damascus was then and still is the capital of Syria. It is located in a fertile oasis a few miles northeast of Mount Hermon, and is surrounded on the south, east, and north by desert. Several rivers flow by the city (most notably the Amana [modern El-Barada] and Pharpar [modern El-Awaj]; see 2 Kings 5:12). These provide an abundance of water for the cultivation of crops of all kinds. And the "Street called Straight" still runs east-to-west through the city.[7]

With the needed authorization in his possession, Saul began the 150 mile, six day journey from Jerusalem to Damascus. Around noon (22:6) on the last day of his journey, and with the possibility of being in Damascus by nightfall, Saul ignored the time-honored custom of taking a siesta. All of a sudden a blinding light from heaven flashed around him, and he fell to the ground. Later, in describing the event, he stated that the light was brighter than the midday sun (26:13). While prostate on the dusty road he heard a voice asking, "Saul, Saul, why are you persecuting Me?"

In answer, Saul asked, "Who are you, Lord?"

Because he believed Jesus to be dead, he did not know who was speaking to him. To his question, "Who are you?" he received the unexpected reply: "I am Jesus whom you are persecuting."

Most writers spend their time trying to explain the source of the bright light that Saul saw,[8] but according to 1

---

7. See R. K. Harrison, ed., *Major Cities of the Biblical World* (Nashville: Nelson, 1985), 96-106.

Corinthians 9:1 Saul saw the Lord Jesus in His risen glory (cf. 1 Corinthians 15:7-8). Saul had refused to believe the report of Christ's resurrection, but now he realized that not only was the Lord Jesus alive, He was vitally identified with His followers. Saul's persecution of Christians was also persecution of Israel's Messiah. In that instant he realized how wrong he had been to oppose the teaching of Christ's followers.

Some Bible scholars try to explain the bright light Saul saw as a physiological phenomenon. They claim that Saul was an epileptic and had a seizure. Luke, who wrote of Saul's experience, was a medical doctor and he did not believe that there was a medical explanation for what occurred. Others offer a variety of naturalistic explanations. One of the most widely accepted views advances the theory that what Saul saw was a flash of lightening,[9] and when he knocked his head on the ground he thought he heard someone speak to him.

But there is a better explanation, *viz.*, the Shekinah glory (cf. Hebrews 1:3) that occurs whenever God begins a new phase in His redemptive purpose. Stephen tells us that

---

8. An extensive discussion of the different theories has been provided by P. J. Gloag, *A Critical and Exegetical Commentary on the Acts of the Apostles*, 2 vols. (Minneapolis: Klock and Klock, 1979), I:318-21.
9. W. Barclay, *The Acts of the Apostles* (Philadelphia: Westminster, 1955), 72. Such a view contradicts Acts 9:27 (note, however, that when Barnabas brought Paul to the apostles he described to them *how Saul had seen the Lord* .... See also Galatians 1:11-12; Ephesians 3:3).

when God turned from dealing with the nations in general He appeared in all His glory to Abraham (7:2), and told him that through him and his descendants "all the families of the earth would be blessed" (Genesis 12:3). He intended for Abraham and his descendants to be a kingdom of priests and be the means whereby the message of salvation would spread to the nations (Exodus 19:6). This marked a new phase in His progressive revelation.[10]

And when God again planned a departure from the past that involved taking the gospel to Gentiles (Galatians 3:14), He manifested Himself to Saul in His risen glory. He also commissioned him to be a witness to what he had seen and heard (26:16-18; Galatians 1:15-16).[11]

Saul, in recounting this event, consistently attributed what happened to the appearance of the Lord Jesus in His heavenly glory (22:6-11; 26:13-18; 1 Corinthians 9:1)[12].

---

10. Previously Abraham's family had been idolaters (Joshua 24:2-3, note 2*b* where we read that *"They served other gods"*), but when the Lord appeared to him he was turned from darkness to light and came to understand the power of God.
11. The light, "Shekinah," is a word not found in Scripture but is used by later Jews and by Christians to express the visible divine Presence.
12. J. R. W. Stott, *The Spirit, The Church, and the World* (Downers Grove, IL: InterVarsity, 1990), 169-73, describes the way in which Paul's heart was prepared to receive what took place on the Damascus highway.

The vision left him blind, and those who were with him had to lead him by the hand the rest of the way to Damascus.

A Man With A Special Commission

The scene now shifts to the home of Ananias. He was not one of the rich and powerful people in Damascus, nor was he among the movers and shakers in the local church. Yet his influence was felt, for years later Saul portrayed him as one who was "devout by the standard of the Law, and well spoken of by all the Jews who lived" in Damascus (22:12).

As we ponder in our minds the kind of person Ananias was, an important question arises and it demands an answer: Why did the Lord Jesus seek out Ananias?

There is something of great importance in the answer to this question. Ananias was not the pastor of the church, nor was he one of the elected officials. But he had certain traits that made him indispensable for the task at hand: he was humble, obedient, and sensitive to the needs of others. Today the task of bringing someone as important as Saul into the fold would have been assigned to a person of equal rank who would lend an element of dignity to the task. That is the way we think and act. The Lord Jesus shows us, however, that anyone in the church can be used if he or she is modest, obedient, and compassionate.

Ananias possessed these characteristics, and the Lord chose him. He was an ordinary man who lived his faith amid the ordinary circumstances of his work-a-day world. And the very ordinariness of his life provides a fitting pattern for many Christians today, particularly if they feel that their circumstances keep them in obscurity.

The ordinary life is often the most difficult. It has fewer outward stimuli, and therefore requires a deeper commitment to the teaching of Scripture if it is to be consistent. What is often overlooked is that God uses those who are grounded in the truths of Scripture and courageous enough to live for the Lord in a quiet, unobtrusive way. In the end, those whom the Lord finds "faithful over few things" will be rewarded by being given responsibility over many things (Matthew 25:21ff.).

As a result of Ananias' adherence to the teaching of Scripture, he was honest in his business dealings, and people trusted him. His reputation for integrity and reliability had been gained over many years of consistent living, and when he became a follower of the Lord Jesus the same piety and devotion characterized his life as a Christian.

But how would Ananias respond to Christ's instruction to go to Saul so that he could receive his sight?

We are not told where Ananias was when the Lord Jesus appeared to him in a vision. Perhaps it was during the afternoon siesta. All we know is that the Lord said to him, "Get up and go to the street called Straight, and inquire at the house of Judas for a man from Tarsus named Saul, for he is praying, and he has seen in a vision a man named Ananias come in and lay his hands on him, so that he might regain his sight" (9:11-12).

It was both natural and understandable for Ananias to question what he heard. He was not a mindless robot. Instead of trying to sidestep Christ's orders, his response shows his submission as well as his caution. He replied, "Lord, I have heard from many about this man, how much harm he did to Your saints at Jerusalem; and here he has authority from the chief priests to bind all who call on Your name" (9:13-14).

If Ananias had been *living in our day*, his response might have been different. He would probably have shown far less respect, and might have said ....

> But Lord, why me? Why do You want me to do this? I'm not the pastor. Tell him to go to Saul. We pay him to do this kind of thing. Or ...
>
> Lord, it may have escaped Your attention, but we have a committee to interview new members. If Saul is to become a part of the church, the committee should first interview him to determine his worthiness. Or ...
>
> Lord, at this point in time, we have no means of determining if Saul's conversion is real. This might be a ruse to find out who the Christians are. It would then be easy for him to arrest us and take us to Jerusalem for trial and execution. Or ...
>
> Lord, You know me. I'm not a brave man. If my wife knew that I was even thinking of undertaking such a task she'd kill me and save Saul the trouble."

The Lord Jesus responded to Ananias' concerns by saying, "Go, for he is a chosen instrument of Mine, to bear My name before the Gentiles and kings and the sons of Israel; for I will show him how much he must suffer for My name's sake" (9:15-16).

And with that assurance Ananias got up and went to look for Saul. He did not procrastinate, but willingly obeyed the Lord's instructions. He found the house in which Saul was staying, and was shown into the room where he was praying. "And after laying his hands on him, he said, 'Brother Saul, the Lord Jesus, who appeared to you on the road by which you were coming here, has sent me so that you may regain your sight and be filled with the Holy Spirit'" (9:17-18).

Ananias' self-effacing humility and compassion are evident. He did not mention himself or his membership in the church. Instead, he laid his hands on Saul signifying his identification with him, and he confirmed Saul's acceptance into the community of faith by referring to him as "Brother." The Lord Jesus had not told Ananias to do or say these things. His words and deeds show what was in his heart.

The scales immediately fell from Saul's eyes, and he regained his sight. He then got up and was baptized (possibly in one of Damascus' rivers) to further show his identification with the Lord and His people. After that he broke his fast.

This is a great story describing how Saul, who later evangelized much of Asia Minor (modern Turkey) and Europe, was welcomed into the church.

THE GOSPEL OF OUR SALVATION

Saul's conversion does not fit our mold of how conversions ought to take place. He did not respond to an "altar call" or repeat the "sinner's prayer." On the surface his conversion seems to have been unexpected, even forced upon him.

God's grace, however, was not sudden, but neither was it compulsive. Although Saul was unaware of it, the Holy Spirit had been preparing his heart for some time. All of this is evident in Christ's words to Saul, "Is it hard for you to kick against the pricks?" (26:14, KJV). The pricks of the goad had been many and may have included the brave death of Stephen when he asked the Lord to forgive his murderers; his own inner turmoil over the failure of Jewish legalism to bring him any inner peace; and the nagging doubts he had about the miracles Jesus had performed. All of this would have caused him deep unrest. Though he believed himself to be faultless (Philippians 3:5-7), he knew his righteousness was external and that his thoughts and motives did not fit him for God's presence (cf. Romans 7:7-12). He tried to ease his tortured conscience with more intense persecutions of the church, but peace eluded him. Like Francis Thompson in *The Hound of Heaven*, he fled from the Lord.

"I fled [from] Him down the nights and down the days;
I fled [from] Him down the arches of the years;
I fled [from] Him down the labyrinthine ways, ... [and]
I hid from Him ....
[only to fall] precipitated,
down Titanic glooms of chasmed fears ....

And Stephen's murder must have left a deep impression on him, for in the end Saul found that all he did to gain peace and happiness was only vanity and a striving after the wind (cf. Ecclesiastes 1:2; 12:8). At last he was brought to a point in his experience when he confessed himself to be "of all man's clotted clay the dingiest clot" (cf. 1 Corinthians 15:9). He humbly submitted to Christ's love and grace, and found the peace he had looked for for so long.

John Owen is remembered as one of the great stalwarts of the Christian church. Few, however, know how he came to Christ. When Owen was a student at Oxford he began to seek earnestly for peace. One day he learned that the great Dr. Edmund Calamy would be preaching at Aldermanbury Chapel in London. He journeyed down to London hoping to find rest for his troubled soul. Imagine his disappointment when Dr. Calamy cancelled at the last minute and an unknown stranger from the country was pressed into service.

This young disciple of the Lord took as his text "Why are you fearful, O you of little faith." His message touched John Owen's heart and he left that chapel trusting in Christ for his soul's salvation. He made a diligent effort to find out who the young man was, but no one at Aldermanbury

Chapel knew him. John Owen went on to graduate from Oxford and held several Free Church pastorates before being invited back to Oxford as dean of Christ Church College.

Most of us are like that unknown country preacher who never knew what great service he performed that Sunday morning. We are not numbered among the wise or the learned or the debaters of world affairs, but in the providence of God, we may, like Ananias, influence some future leader of the church.

CHAPTER TWO

THE MAN WHO WAS MISTAKEN FOR A GOD

People in the Greek world believed that, on occasion, their gods left the splendors of Mount Olympus, came to earth, and walked incognito among the people. The purpose was to see firsthand who worshiped them and gave them gifts. The Roman poet Ovid[13] (43 B.C.–A.D. 18) told of Jupiter and Mercury (the Latin names for Zeus and Hermes) who came to an old couple named Philemon and Baucis who lived in the hills of Phrygia near Lystra. This couple was very poor, but they entertained the two men, never realizing that they were gods appearing in human form.

Before the gods left they took Philemon and Baucis outside the city, and told them that because the people in the town had treated them so gruffly and refused them hospitality, the city was to be destroyed. The gods then caused the city to sink into the earth, leaving the old couple the sole survivors. The gods then asked Philemon and Baucis what they wanted most in all the world. This couple requested to be allowed to become the priest and priestess of the new temple that appeared miraculously where their old house had been, and asked that when they died they would be together so that neither would be left alone without the

---

13. Ovid, *Metamorphoses* 8:620-724. See also W. M. Calder, *Expositor* 7, 10 (1910), 1-6.

other. And so it happened. When they died, they were standing together, and the gods caused them to be miraculously transformed into a tree with two stems coming from the single trunk.

This legend was widely circulated about one hundred years before the arrival of Paul and Barnabas in Lystra, and it explains why the people were so anxious not to repeat the mistake of the past. So, when Paul healed the man who suffered from a congenital defect and could not walk, the Lystrans concluded that the gods had paid them a visit (14:8-18). They identified Paul with Hermes because he was the chief spokesman, and Barnabas they believed to be Zeus. *And that is how Barnabas was mistaken for a god.*

In earlier times the Greeks had described Zeus as "the Thunderer," "the Cloud-gatherer," the "Lord of Lightning." Later on he was portrayed in more relational terms as an avenger of wrongs, the giver of victory, the protector of oaths, the guardian of the rights and privileges of hosts and guests, and the counselor who by a nod of his immortal head granted the prayer of suppliants. Statues portray Zeus as tall, well-proportioned, and good looking.

Some years ago, when my family and I were in Ephesus where I acquired a head of Zeus that had been dug up by an archaeologist. It had been broken off the body, and the events that led to it being buried are unknown. It lay unseen until the spade of an archaeologist unearthed it. He or she wasn't too careful, for the tip of Zeus' nose was chipped off.

Now no one knows what Zeus looked like, for he was a mythical figure. This archaeological artifact, however, does represent him as a handsome individual, and this would fit in with the writings of Homer and others who portrayed him as tall and statuesque in his bearing-- and from this we deduce that Barnabas shared these same attributes.

Of course, if Barnabas was handsome, the question arises, "What of Paul? What was he like?" Here, if we are to believe tradition, we face disappointment. In a non-canonical work entitled *The Acts of Paul and Thecla*, Paul is described as short, bowlegged, baldheaded, with meeting eyebrows, and a long nose.[14]

As we focus our attention on Barnabas[15] it will be of help to us if we consider his ministry in three areas: (1) His ministry in Jerusalem, (2) His ministry in Antioch, and (3) His ministry on the first missionary journey.

---

14. This description comes from Sir William M. Ramsay's *The Church in the Roman Empire Before A.D. 170* (London: Hodder & Stoughton, 1893), 31-32. For a translation of *The Acts of Paul and Thecla*, see pages 375-442. A briefer version may be found in J. H. Moulton's, *From Egyptian Rubbish-Heaps* (London: C. H. Kelly, 1916, 50-77). Cf. The Corinthians description of Paul's physical appearance as "unimpressive" (2 Corinthians 10:10).
15. Acts 4:36-37; 9:27; 11:22-30; 12:25; 13:1-14; 15:1-40; 1Corinthians 9:6; Galatians 2:1, 9, 13; Colossians 4:10.

Ministry in Jerusalem

But what do we know of Barnabas apart from the fact that he was probably tall and good looking? The Greeks placed their emphasis on externals, whereas the early believers prized internal qualities. We note, therefore, that Barnabas was considered to be a good man, and full of the Holy Spirit and of faith through whom considerable numbers were brought to the Lord. (11:24).

To adequately study the character of any man we need to take into account, not only the distinguishing features of his own mind and disposition, but also circumstances of every kind by which he was surrounded.[16] We note, therefore, that Barnabas was a Jewish Levite from Cyprus. At birth he had been given the name Joseph (4:36*a*). We are not told when he came to Judah or how he came to faith in the Lord Jesus as his Savior. We do know that following the establishment of the church in Jerusalem he apparently spent his time helping and encouraging those Jews who had been put out of the synagogues following their confession of Christ (see 11:23-24; cf. 13:43). His ministry must have been so winsome that the apostles gave him the nickname "Barnabas" (*bar*, "son of," *nabas*, "encouragement or exhortation").[17]

---

16. Cf. J. S. Howson, *The Companions of St. Paul* (New York: American Tract Society, n.d.), 7.

Then when the Jewish leaders deprived Christian widows of the support they had received from the Temple (cf. 6:1-7), those in the church who had ample means could alleviate their privation. Some who had land sold it and gave the proceeds to the apostles so that distribution could be made to those who were impoverished.[18] Barnabas, who felt the same sense of oneness as the others, sold the land he owned on the island of Cyprus, and gave the entire proceeds to the apostles (4:37). Luke's use of the singular *to chrema*, "the money," indicates that Barnabas gave the entire proceeds from the sale to the apostles.[19] His gift was truly sacrificial, for later on in his ministry he had to work with his hands to support himself (1 Corinthians 9:6).

---

17. Nicknames sometimes replaced given names as in the case of Gaius. He was the son of the Roman general, Germanicus, and accompanied his father on his campaigns. Though very young, he and was given a uniform like the other officers (including boots), and accompanied his father everywhere. The soldiers gave him the nickname "Caligula," or "little boots," and this stuck to him even when he was made emperor. See Tacitus, *Annals* 1:41, 69; and DioCassius, [Works] 57:5. Even today the history books refer to him as Caligula.

18. Some writers have referred to this action as a "Christian communism." The term is misleading. The practice was voluntary and its practice limited to those within the Jerusalem Church. The State played no part in it. And there is no indication in Scripture that this practice was ever intended to become normative among all churches.

19. This contrasts forcefully with Acts 5:1-11.

Sometime after these events Saul, who had been living and ministering in Damascus, came to Jerusalem (9:26ff; Galatians 1:18). He naturally wanted to associate with the believers, but they were afraid of him. Memories of the way in which he had persecuted the church were still fresh in their minds, and their fears were understandable.

Barnabas showed himself to be a true "son of encouragement" for he reached out to and befriended Saul (9:26-27). There are some who believe that he and Saul were old friends, having studied together in the University of Tarsus,[20] but there is no biblical warrant for such an imaginative theory. What is impressed on us as we read the story is that Barnabas was free from the kind of stifling pettiness that follows a strict and often excessive adherence to the law. He set aside the trivialities of hair-splitting with its unimportant limitations, reached out to Saul and befriended him when he was most in need of the trust of a fellow Christian.

As Barnabas met with Saul his spirit witnessed with Saul's spirit that the one-time persecutor of the church had indeed become a child of God. He introduced Saul to the apostles and described to them how he had seen the Lord on the road to Damascus, and that the Lord Jesus had talked to him. He also explained how in Damascus Saul had spoken boldly in the name of the Lord.

---

20. Cf. H. C. Lees, *St. Paul's Friends* (London: Religious Tract Society, 1918), 17; and J. A. Robertson, *Hidden Romance of the New Testament* (London: J. Clarke, 1920), 46-61.

Saul stayed in Jerusalem, and moved about freely in the city (9:27-28; Galatians 1:18-19). History, however, was soon to repeat itself. He had been forced to secretly leave Damascus to save his life (9:23-25), and after only fifteen days in Jerusalem he faced the same situation (Galatians 1:18). Some Hellenistic (i.e., Greek-speaking) Jews[21] stirred up trouble and Saul was compelled to flee for his life. Christians in Jerusalem brought him down to Caesarea and sent him to Tarsus (9:31).[22]

In summing up Barnabas' ministry to Saul, the late Herbert S. Seekings wrote, "He possessed that rare gift of insight which enables men to get beneath the surface and discover the depths of another's soul; and often in the face of popular prejudice [to be] courageous enough to act" in spite of hostile sentiment.[23]

Ministry in Antioch

At this point Luke provides some historic background so that we can better understand the spread of the gospel. He records that those who had been forced to leave Jerusalem on account of persecution went throughout the surrounding countries preaching the gospel to Jews (11:19; cf. 7:1ff.). Some, however, from Cyprus and Cyrene, began minister-

---

21. W. M. Ramsay, *The Cities of St. Paul* (London: Hodder & Stoughton, 1907), 30-42.
22. Ibid., 85-235.
23. Seekings, *The Men of the Pauline Circle*, 36.

ing to Greeks (11:20) who lived in Antioch-on-the-Orontes River (also known as Syrian Antioch to distinguish it from Pisidian Antioch).[24] When the church in Jerusalem heard of this they sent Barnabas to investigate, for these Greeks had not first become proselytes.

The Jerusalem church's choice of Barnabas to check the orthodoxy of this new movement shows the confidence they placed in him. The assignment called for considerable wisdom and tact.

When Barnabas arrived in Antioch "and witnessed the grace of God, he rejoiced and began to encourage them all with resolute heart to remain true to the Lord ... and a considerable number were brought" to faith in Christ (11:23-24). In this we see that Barnabas was free from the parochialism and narrow provincialism that often characterizes people who occupy important ecclesiastical positions.

While Barnabas remained in Antioch, the rapid growth of the work soon made it necessary for someone to help him. But who would be the best person for this vital ministry? The one individual whose name immediately came to mind was Saul. But where was he? All Barnabas knew was that he had been involved in "church planting" in the area of Tarsus (Galatians 1:21).

---

24. Harrison, ed.., *Major Cities of the Biblical World*, 8-20. This city was founded about 300 B.C. by Seleucus I Nicator ("The Conqueror") and named after his father, Antiochus. It was the third largest city in the area, and considered by many to be the most prominent and also the most beautiful.

Barnabas left Antioch for Tarsus *to seek for Saul* (11:25). The verb translated "seek" implies difficulty in finding the object (usually a person).[25] This shows that Saul had not been idle in the ten years since leaving Jerusalem.

When Saul learned of the work Barnabas had been doing in Antioch he gladly accompanied him there, and a very fruitful year of ministry followed. So significant was their work that it could neither be classified as Jewish or Gentile, and this led the people of Antioch to refer to the believers by the name "Christian" (11:26).

In the course of time some teachers from Jerusalem came to Antioch. One of them, a man named Agabus, predicted a severe famine throughout the Roman world.[26] The believers in Antioch immediately began collecting money for their fellow-believers in Jerusalem, and their gift was sent in care of Barnabas and Saul (11:29-30).

25. J. H. Moulton and G. Milligan, *Vocabulary of the Greek Testament* (London: Hodder & Stoughton, 1952), 32. The difficulty of Barnabas' search is further underscored by the words "*and when he had found him*" (11:26). Furthermore, the letter the Jerusalem church later sent to the church in Antioch mentions "the brethren who are of the Gentiles in Antioch and Syria and Cilicia ..." (15:23). Where did these churches come from (cf. Galatians 1:21)? The obvious answer is that they were started by Paul.

26. The use of *oikoumene*, the "inhabited earth", in certain contexts is coterminous with the empire. The Jewish historian, Josephus, confirms the accuracy of this prediction by writing of a great famine in the reign of the emperor Claudius (see his *Antiquities of the Jews*, XX:2:5; cf. XX:5:2, III:15:3).

Barnabas had an aunt named Mary who was living in Jerusalem, and he and Saul probably lodged with her. She had a son named Mark, and when Barnabas and Saul returned to Antioch they took Mark with them (12:25).

Some indication of the division of labor within the church in Antioch is indicated by the fact that the church had five "prophets and teachers" (13:1). Because the Scriptures were not complete, God gave to the church "prophets" through whom the Holy Spirit made known His will and message to the people. One day while they were praying He indicated that Barnabas and Saul should be set apart for a special ministry (13:2).

Ministry on the First Missionary Journey

In obedience to the will of the Lord the leaders of the church laid their hands on Barnabas and Saul and dismissed them to take up their new work. And so began the first missionary journey (13:1–14:28). It is important to note that the Holy Spirit mentioned Barnabas first, identifying him as the leader (13:7).

The laying on of hands was not an ordination of Barnabas and Saul (cf. Galatians 1:1; 2:6), but a sign of the church's identification or oneness with them in the special work they would he doing.

Barnabas and Saul took Mark with them as their "helper" (13:5). The word is *hyperetes,* meaning "servant or assistant," but it does not tell us whether Mark's service was pastoral (e.g., baptizing or instructing new converts) or practical (e.g., cooking, cleaning, making travel arrangements). The word is also used of an "under-rower" on a trireme ship.

Barnabas and those with him sailed to Cyprus, landing at Salamis. Barnabas, it will be remembered, was from Cyprus, and he had friends and relatives on the island. It was natural for him to want them to hear the gospel.

The ministry of Barnabas and Saul took them from one end of the island to the other, and when they arrived in Paphos they were invited to speak with the proconsul, a man named Sergius Paulus. As they were sharing the gospel with him a false prophet named Bar-Jesus opposed them. He was silenced by Saul in a most decisive way. The result was that the proconsul came to faith in Christ (13:6-11).

From this time on Saul came to be known as Paul–a most appropriate change inasmuch as the missionaries now worked in a predominately Gentile environment. But this was not the only change that occurred. In 13:13 we read of "Paul and his company" (see also 13:9, 43, 46, 50), and it is evident that he was now the acknowledged leader. How did Barnabas adjust to this transition in leadership? Apparently Barnabas' identity was not invested in positions of prominence or prestige. He was intent on serving the Lord, and could do so whether he was the leader of the missionary band or merely an associate.

Next Paul's party sailed to Perga, a coastal town in Pamphilia in what is today modern Turkey. There John left them and returned to Jerusalem. The apostles journeyed inland and came at length to Pisidian Antioch. Paul preached in the local synagogue, but when some of the Jews saw the large crowds that attended his ministry, they became jealous and vehemently opposed him (13:45). Persecution followed, and the missionaries were compelled to leave the city.

The next city they entered was Iconium (14:1-6). Here they narrowly escaped stoning, and leaving the province of Galatia fled to the province of Lyconia taking refuge in Lystra. Paul and Barnabas believed that in this remote, mountainous region they would be safe. But Jewish legalists from Antioch and Iconium pursued them, and incited the volatile crowd. This resulted in Paul being stoned, dragged outside the city and left for dead (14:19-20). To the amazement of the disciples, however, he got up and reentered the city.

After this the missionaries ministered in Derbe before beginning to retrace their steps. They returned to each city in which they had preached the gospel, and strengthening the believers. They also appointed elders in each church. They then took a ship and returned to Syrian Antioch where they reported to the church all the things the Lord had done.

They spent a long time in Antioch (14:28). After several years Paul suggested to Barnabas that they again visit the churches they had established. When Barnabas wanted to take Mark with them, a sharp disagreement (*paroxysm*) ensued (15:37-40). Paul felt strongly that Mark was unfit for the ministry. The two leaders found no common ground-- and ever since the church has debated who was right.

As we review the situation we need to keep in mind that Paul was a theologian, and a forceful speaker. He loved to argue with those who disagreed with him (9:28-29, etc; see 19:8 NIV) and he reacted strongly against taking John Mark with them, believing that he had shown himself unreliable on their first journey. As Dr. H. A. W. Meyer has remarked, "*Fickleness* in the service of Christ was to Paul's bold and decided strength of character a ... foreign element, with which he could not enter into any union either abstractly or for the sake of public example."[27]

The church at Antioch sided with Paul and committed Paul and Silas to the grace of God (15:40). Soon thereafter they left Antioch and traveled through Syria and Cilicia strengthening the churches earlier established by Paul.

Barnabas was more gracious and gentle than Paul, and believed that Mark should be given a second chance. He, therefore, took Mark and sailed for Cyprus. Had he not done so we might not have had our second gospel!

It is significant that neither Barnabas nor Paul suggested that they pray over their disagreement. And neither sought the will of the Lord in private. Instead, they parted company.

In retrospect, the church needs leaders like Paul and Barnabas who can work together. Paul was a forceful task-oriented leader, whereas Barnabas as a relational leader.

---

27. H. A. W. Meyer, *Critical and Exegetical Handbook to the Acts of the Apostles* (New York: Funk & Wagnalls, 1889), 298.

Both are essential to the life of the church. Barnabas did not covet the "No. 1" position, and in this he was like the Lord Jesus of whom Paul later wrote in Philippians 2:3-7.

As we sum up Barnabas' traits we find that he stands out as one of the choicest saints in the early church. He had a gracious personality, a generous disposition, and an intuitive insight into the needs of the human heart. He excelled in building bridges, and lived his life above the narrowness and pettiness of his times. He was always ready to help the needy, and though he had shortcomings like other men, he sought out the best in those whom he met.

CHAPTER THREE

THE POWER OF ENCOURAGEMENT

If you were to ask the people of the church you attend to give a "Yes" or "No" answer to the question, "Is there hope for a person who has turned his back on the Lord?" what responses would you receive? And what Scriptures might they cite in support of their view?

It is true that the Bible offers certain warnings, but in this age of grace forgiveness is possible (cf. Matthew 12:31-32). An illustration of God's lovingkindness and restoration is to be found in the Bible's teaching about a young man named John Mark.[28]

Because John Mark's ministry was intimately connected with that of his cousin Barnabas, there is an unavoidable overlap in this chapter in treating the details of his life.

A Good Heritage

John Mark is first introduced to us as a resident of Jerusalem. He is referred to as "John who was also called Mark" (12:12). John was his Jewish name and, following the custom of the day, he took a Latin *pronomen*, Mark. *The usage of these names by the biblical writer provides a key to*

---

28. See Mark 14:13-14, 51-52; Acts 12:12, 25; 13:5, 13; 15:36-39; Colossians 4:10; 2 Timothy 4:11; Philemon 1:24; 1 Peter 5:13.

our understanding of how he responded to different situations.

John may have been born on the island of Cyprus and come to the mainland while still a child. He was reared in Jerusalem and benefitted from a thorough religious training both at home and under the rabbis in the local synagogue. He also profited from a good education, being fluent in Aramaic, Greek and perhaps Latin.

Because there is no mention of any brothers or sisters we conclude that John was an only child.

From references in the book of Acts we presume that his parents were wealthy. They owned a spacious home with a large upper room where tradition tells us the Lord Jesus and His disciples ate the "Last Supper." And in all probability it was in their home that upwards of one hundred and twenty people met together for prayer after Christ's ascension (1:14-15).

During John's youth a spirit of expectation swept over the land. A young desert preacher who was also named John (who is known to us as John the Baptist), and who looked like the prophet Elijah, began preaching to people traveling along the dusty caravan routes. These travelers would invariably stop for water and a rest at a ford along the bank of the River Jordan, and there this young prophet would call upon them to repent of their sins because the Kingdom of heaven was soon to appear. His method of presentation was unlike the prescriptive teaching of the Pharisees who emphasized the need to keep their traditions–something which their numerous additions to the law made it increasingly hard for people to do.

A few months later the Lord Jesus came to the River Jordan and was baptized by John. When He began His ministry He did so by cleansing the Temple (John 2:13-16). This aroused the ire of the religious leaders, and they kept on trying to discredit Him in the eyes of the people.

John Mark's parents may have heard the Lord Jesus preach when He visited Jerusalem for one of the feasts[29] (Exodus 23:14-17). When and by what means they placed their trust in Him as the Messiah is not known. One thing is certain, their profession of faith in the Lord Jesus added a new dimension to the training of their son.

A few years passed. Then, with the approach of the Feast of Passover, events began to move rapidly toward a climax. Tradition is virtually unanimous that it was in the home of John Mark's parents that the Lord Jesus and His disciples celebrated the feast. In Mark 14:13-15 (cf. Luke 22:10-12) we are told that the Lord Jesus sent two of His disciples into the city to prepare the place where He and His disciples would remember God's deliverance of His people from bondage in Egypt. He said to them,

---

29. Eusebius of Caesarea (c. 260–c. 340) quotes Papias who stated that Mark never heard the Lord Jesus personally (*Eusebius: The Church History*, trans. P. L. Maier [Grand Rapids: Kregel, 1999],129). But this statement can be misleading, for the context of Papias' remark has to do with Mark's record of Peter's reminiscences.

"Go into the city, and a man will meet you carrying a pitcher of water; follow him; and wherever he enters, say to the owner of the house, 'The Teacher says, 'Where is My guest room in which I may eat the Passover with My disciples?' And he himself will show you a large upper room furnished and ready; prepare for us there."

The instructions of the Lord Jesus reveal His foreknowledge. The man who showed the disciples the upper room must have been John's father (the *oikedespotei*, "master of the house"), and the young man carrying the pitcher of water was most likely John. If this is not a reference to John then the incident would have been passed over as unimportant. Carrying water for the needs of a household was considered woman's work, and for a young man to be doing this was totally unexpected. The servants in the house were probably busy making preparations for the Passover and so John's mother asked her son to fetch some water from the village well.

It seems likely that after completing the Passover meal, when the Lord Jesus and His disciples left for the Garden of Gethsemane, John heard their muffled voices and footsteps on the outer staircase and decided to follow them. Hastily wrapping a *sindona*, or light cloak around him,[30] he followed the Lord Jesus and His disciples across the Kidron

---

30. H. B. Swete, *The Gospel According to St. Mark* (Grand Rapids; Eerdmans, 1956), 354. Swete connects the *sindona* with the outer garment left in the hands of Potiphar's wife when Joseph ran from her presence (cf. Genesis 39:12ff.).

valley to the Mount of Olives and the Garden of Gethsemane. There he would have overheard Christ's prayer. Then, when Judas and the soldiers came to arrest the Lord Jesus, he would have seen the disciples flee into the darkness. He was the only one who remained as an eyewitness of the events that followed.

Though this *neaviskos*, "young man," is unnamed, it could only have been John (Mark 14:51-52), for had it been some one else there would have been no reason to record the incident.

After Christ's crucifixion, resurrection and ascension, the home of John's parents became the center of activity. The leading men of the church came there for prayer and fellowship, and it was in the upper room that the apostles and about one hundred and twenty of Christ's followers waited for the coming of the Holy Spirit (1:13-14, 15*b*).

It was also in John's home that he met with and listened to the leaders of the early church, and his relationship with Peter led ultimately to his conversion (1 Peter 5:13*b*).

During these years John's home was not immune from sadness. From Acts 12:12, where the residence is referred to as the "house of Mary," we are left to conclude that sometime after Passover and Pentecost John's father died. Mary seems to have been a very capable person, but with the passing of her husband it would have been natural for more and more responsibility to be delegated to her son. And so John's home, that had given him moral strength and spiritual awareness, now equipped him with administrative experience.

The early days of the church were exciting ones. The Holy Spirit was at work in the hearts of the people, and conversions occurred daily. It is also likely that Barnabas was a frequent visitor in Mary's home. When a new work was started in Antioch-on-the-Orontes Barnabas was commissioned to go there and give leadership where needed. Then, when the famine broke out, he and Paul brought relief from the believers in Antioch to their fellow-Christians in Jerusalem. This visit gave John the opportunity to renew his acquaintance with Barnabas (11:27-29).

It was at this time that Herod arrested James, the leader of the church, and had him beheaded. This pleased the Jews, and so he arrested Peter as well (12:1-4). The church met for prayer in Mary's home, and when Peter was miraculously released from prison (12:5-17) the believers rejoiced. These events must have had a powerful impact on John.

When Barnabas was ready to return to Antioch he suggested that John accompany him. Like most mothers, Mary would have been reluctant to lose the companionship of her son, but she probably realized that this was a great opportunity for him, and so did not stand in his way.

And for a whole year John worked with Barnabas and Paul in Antioch.

The Chance of a Lifetime

From this time onwards John is most often referred to as Mark.[31] We do not know what duties he performed in Antioch, but inasmuch as there was a large Jewish population in the city, Mark may have contented himself with work among them. When the Holy Spirit called Barnabas and Paul to begin work in a different area (13:1ff.), Barnabas' first thought was to take Mark along with them. And so Mark was privileged to take part in the first missionary journey.

Barnabas and Paul traveled to Cilicia where they took a ship bound for Cyprus (13:1-4). Scripture records, "And they *also* had John as their attendant" (13:5).[32] The inclusion of the word "also" has led some Bible scholars to believe that John helped with the preaching. Luke's reference to him as "John" in the context of ministry in the synagogue would lead us to conclude that Barnabas and Paul felt comfortable with him ministering to Jews.

Mark is also described as the "attendant" who carried out specific tasks for Barnabas and Paul. The word "attendant"originally meant "under-rower" on a Roman trireme (i.e., ship with three rows of oars). Later on the word came to mean "one who serves a superior." Exactly how Mark served Barnabas and Paul is uncertain. In addition to teaching, he may also have baptized and instructed new converts, arranged for accommodation, and made plans for travel.[33]

---

31. *Epiklethenta*, "called," is an aorist passive participle pointing to a singular act.
32. H. B. Hackett, *A Commentary on the Acts of the Apostles*, new ed., ed. A. Hovey and E. Abbot (Philadelphia: American Baptist Publication Society, 1882), 151. John's activities, however, must also be interpreted in light of the fact that he was the "helper" of Paul and Barnabas.

The missionary party traversed the entire island of Cyprus from Salamis to Paphos. At Paphos they encountered a Jewish sorcerer named Bar-jesus (13:6-11), and Mark witnessed anew the power of God working through Paul. The missionaries spent some time in Paphos, but when they left a change had taken place in the leadership of the small group. They were now spoken of as "the ones around (or with) Paul" (13:13). Barnabas was no longer the leader.

We can only speculate on how this change in leadership affected Mark. What were his feelings as he began to see Paul dominate each discussion and make decisions. Is it possible that under Barnabas' kindly supervision he had responded willingly to whatever he was asked to do, whereas Paul may have been harsher, more task-oriented, and more demanding?

We have no means of knowing how Mark felt as they sailed to the coastline of what is today Turkey. One thing we do know: When they arrived at Perga in the province of Pamphilia and began planning a trip into the interior "*John left them and returned to Jerusalem*" (13:13). Luke gives no reason for Mark's departure other than his use of John's Jewish name.

The reason or reasons for Mark's departure have intrigued the church down through the ages. Some have thought that he was homesick. Others believe that he based his decision to return to Jerusalem on the change of leader-

---

33. R. B. Rackham, *The Acts of the Apostles* (Grand Rapids: Baker, 1964), 199.

ship that had occurred. If, however, their original plan was to preach in cities on the way to Ephesus, then Mark could have responded to a change in their itinerary in the same way Barnabas did. Still others are of the opinion that Paul and Mark succumbed to malaria in Perga,[34] and that is why Paul changed their original plans and decided to journey into the highlands. And others have concluded that Mark, having been reared in well-to-do circumstances, was unfit for arduous missionary travel. Coupled with this view is the fact that the mountains were infested with robbers, and fear of them may have caused him to turn back (cf. 2 Corinthians 11:26).[35]

Finally, however, there is the fact that Mark was a strict orthodox Jew, who had consented to work in cosmopolitan areas where devout Jews and cultured Greeks lived side-by-side, and may have drawn the line at working among the barbarians of Galatia. His narrow religious conceptions had not prepared him for such a radical step.[36] In view of this Luke, who is writing of these events, reverts back to using his Jewish name, *John*. Also in favor of accepting this view is the fact that the "sharp disagreement" (15:39) that separated Paul and Barnabas as they contemplated the second missionary journey would not have occurred for any lesser reason.

---

34. Ramsay, *St. Paul the Traveller*, 71.
35. R. C. H. Lenski, *The Interpretation of the Acts of the Apostles* (Minneapolis: Augsburg, 1961), 504, attributes Mark's defection to lack of courage.
36. *International Standard Bible Encyclopedia* (1929), III:1987. See also Seekings, *Men of the Pauline Circle*, 46ff.

In the final analysis, however, decision-making is often a complex matter, and it is possible that each of these circumstances contributed in some way to Mark's final decision.

Mark showed his instability when he deserted his post at a most inopportune time. His decision to return to Jerusalem gave evidence of his immaturity and inadequate staying power. Consequently he was branded a failure. Whatever may have been his mother's reaction, she no doubt felt the sting of disappointment and shared in the stigma that now attached to her son's name.

This leaves us with an important question: Is there any hope for a quitter? Can anything be done to lift a person from the ash heap of personal failure? How can someone who is deficient in his commitment to a cause become a profitable worker?

These and other questions must be answered, for there are many who believe that such evidence of a flaw in one's character causes that person to be disqualified for further service (cf. 1 Corinthians 9:24-27). However, as we read on in the book of Acts we find that John Mark, who faltered and floundered on the first missionary journey became "Mark the profitable servant" during Paul's imprisonment (2 Timothy 4:11).

Return to the Work

When next we read of John Mark, he is in Antioch. We do not know what motivated him to return there and try to live down the shame of his earlier desertion. It is quite possible that in Jerusalem he again came under the influence of Peter. Peter knew what it was like to fail, for he had disowned Christ. He also knew what it was like to be forgiven and restored, and he may have encouraged Mark to try again. The fact that Mark returned to Antioch gives evidence of the awakening of a sense of responsibility. It also indicates his willingness to admit his past failure.

Mark was in Antioch, when Paul and Barnabas returned from the first missionary journey. While people crowded around Paul and listen to him as he recounted the highpoints of their ministry (14:27-28), Mark probably stood in the shadows at the back of the room. During this time Peter arrived, and while his presence would naturally have been an occasion of great blessing, one unfortunate incident occurred which may have brought Mark into Paul's disfavor again. All went well until some Judaisers (i.e., legalistic Jews) from Jerusalem visited the city. They insisted that faith in Christ was insufficient for salvation and that Gentiles had to be circumcised and keep the law of Moses if they were to be saved.[37]

When these orthodox Jews from Jerusalem visited Antioch Peter lapsed back into his old legalistic habits, and no longer ate meals with Gentiles for fear of becoming ceremonially defiled. This aroused the anger of the apostle Paul who refused to permit any distinction between Jews and Gentiles. It is possible that Mark went along with "the rest of the Jews" who sided with Peter (Galatians 2:13). Such defection definitely would have colored Paul's thinking when, a little later on, he suggested to Barnabas that they undertake a second missionary journey. Barnabas agreed and expressed a desire to take Mark along with them. Paul, however, refused. He did not think that the success of the mission should be jeopardized by one who previously had deserted them. The dissension between these two longtime friends became so heated that they separated (15:39-40*a*). Barnabas felt that Mark should be given a second chance and, taking him, sailed for Cyprus. Paul, receiving the blessing of the church (15:40*b*), took Silas and went north into Cilicia and from there to Asia.

What effect did this dispute have on young Mark? We do not know, but it may have caused him to take seriously the work to which he had been assigned. Luke picks up on this, and from this point onwards uses only Mark's Roman name (15:39*b*).

The history of the book of Acts follows Paul, and so we know very little of the activities of Barnabas and Mark. They minister on the island of Cyprus and then go else-

---

37. Judaism may be dated from the Babylonian captivity. In captivity the Jews were separated from their pagan cultic observances and, under Ezra, began to live according to the Scriptures. Pharisees (i.e., separated ones) emerged and gradually developed traditions (known as the "oral law") that replaced the Scriptures in importance. These oral teachings were later compiled in a book called the *Mishnah*. The volume I have used was translated by Herbert Danby and published by Oxford University Press in 1933. See also the work by G. F. Moore, *Judaism in the First Centuries of the Christian Era* ... (Cambridge: Harvard University Press, 1927-30), 3 vols.

where. After about eleven years Barnabas finishes his earthly ministry. Some believe that following Barnabas' death Mark founded the church in Egypt. There is no biblical evidence to support such a claim. We do know from 1 Peter 5:13 that Mark later worked with Peter, and in sending greetings to the churches we find that they are in the same areas that had intimidated Mark on the first missionary journey (cf. 1 Peter 1:1). The mosquitoes still inhabited the coastline, the mountains were just as rugged, robbers still preyed on unsuspecting travelers, and the hardships of the ministry were just as great. Only Mark was different. He had matured personally and theologically.

In the course of time both Paul and Peter were incarcerated in Rome. Paul wrote to Timothy and exhorted him to come to Rome as quickly as possible, and to bring Mark with him because he was "profitable" for the ministry (2 Timothy 4:11). Mark joined Paul in Rome, and when Paul wrote to the believers in Colossae he ended his letter by mentioning those who joined him in sending them greetings. One of these was Mark (Colossians 4:10).

MAKING A COMEBACK

Like Jonah and Peter, Mark was given a second chance. His cousin Barnabas, ever the encourager, helped his young relative overcome his former personal and theological inadequacies. In taking him to Cyprus, the scene of their earlier missionary work, Barnabas helped Mark build on his earlier successes. Where they went once their ministry on Cyprus was over has not been told to us. All we do know is that the two worked together for about eleven years. With Barnabas' death Mark worked with Peter, interpreting for him, and in time became the useful colleague of the apostle Paul when Paul was in prison.

In Rome Mark wrote his gospel in which he describes Jesus Christ as the "Servant of the Lord." His own experiences admirably equipped him for this task.

Mark is presented to us on the pages of the New Testament as a practical, industrious subordinate who never rose to a place of leadership on a par with the apostles. He was content to serve.

There are several important lessons which we learn from a study of Mark's life.

First, Mark's parents may have been too protective of their son, so that he was ill-prepared to face the harsh realities of life. However, they did give him a good education. His administrative gifts took time to develop, and his growth toward maturity may be measured by his acceptance of increasingly difficult tasks.

Most of us may not be greatly gifted, but all of us can make our lives count for God by sticking to the work which we are called to do. Our own maturity is not achieved by a crash course in college, nor can it be obtained in a supermarket. Maturity is obtained only through trial and error, rebuffs and failure; and it comes only to those who are prepared to pick themselves up after they have fallen down and to try again.

Second, from this study we learn the place and importance of timely encouragement. The reason why some people are so lonely is because they sacrificed too many friends in the pursuit of their goal. Peter and Barnabas both exercised a strong influence over Mark. Peter knew what it was like to fail, and encouraged Mark from his own experience. And Barnabas saw in his cousin real potential and guided him along the path of recovery.

CHAPTER FOUR

THE SECOND STRING

Lovers of different sports are familiar with the term "second string." They know how important these players are to the success of the team. They are available to replace or relieve those who started the game. They do not have the prestige of those who were the first to take to the field, but they are vitally important to the outcome of the contest.

The expression "second string" may be traced back to Medieval times. Archers stood in the front line of battle to weaken the opposing army's forces before hand-to-hand combat began. One of an archer's chief fears was that the string of his bow might break. The prudent archer, therefore, insured that he had two strings, and that a soldier stood behind him with the spare string in his hand.

Paul's cord of fellowship with Barnabas had snapped, and Silas[38] became Paul's "second string" in the ministry of the Gospel. The apostle's choice of him seems very appropriate, for Silas, in addition to having dual citizenship,[39]

---

38. See Acts 15:22, 27, 32-34, 40-41; 16:1–17:15; 18:5; 2 Corinthians 1:19; 1 Thessalonians 1:1; 2 Thessalonians 1:1; 1 Peter 5:12. To our surprise the much-touted *Dictionary of Paul and His Letters*, eds. G. F. Hawthorne, R. P. Martin, and D. G. Reid (Downers Grove, IL: InterVarsity, 1993), 1038pp., fails to mention Silas. This gives evidence of the scant attention paid him by NT scholars.

was a faithful follower of the Lord and had gained considerable experience in ministry in Jerusalem.

It is difficult to gain an accurate impression of Silas. In Luke's record of the "perilous times" through which Paul and his companions passed he seems always to stand in the shadows (2 Corinthians 11:26, cf. also 11:23*b*-27).

Two very brief statements help us understand Silas' gifts and abilities. The first was made by the leaders of the church in Jerusalem. They described him as a "prophet" and one of the "leading men among the brethren" (15:22, 32). A "prophet" in Bible times was a person who was able to declare to others the will of the Lord (1 Corinthians 14:3). On occasion it involved predicting the future, but most often a prophet brought into focus the application of the truth of Scripture to people's specific needs. New Testament prophets were those whose unique gifts enabled them to edify others. Silas was such a person.[40]

---

39. The benefits of Roman citizenship have been described by A. N. Sherwin-White in *The Roman Citizenship*, 2d ed. (Oxford: Clarendon, 1973), 496pp.

40. After taking the letter from the Jerusalem Council to the church in Tarsus, Silas probably returned to Jerusalem, only to go back to Tarsus at a later date. Verse 34 is omitted in most ancient manuscripts, and seems to have been inserted by a scribe to explain how Silas was in Tarsus in 15:40 when he was chosen to take part in the Second Missionary journey. The manuscript evidence for verse 34 is weak.

Dr. I. H. Marshall of Aberdeen comments as follows: "Since Silas had previously left Antioch, we must presume either that he returned in the meanwhile, or that Paul sent for him" (see *The Acts of the Apostles,* Tyndale New Testament Commentaries [Grand Rapids: Eerdmans, 1980], 256). And Silas was also a "chief" man among the brethren. This means that he had faithfully discharged the duties delegated to him, and had eventually become a ruler of importance.

But we must not overlook his humility. A lesser man than Silas might have declined the position of Paul's "string-bearer" through ambition and a desire to be in first place.

The second reference to Silas comes from the pen of the Apostle Paul. In his first letter to the new believers in Thessalonica he reminded them how he and Silas had "labored and toiled ... night and day" so that they might not be a burden to anyone. He then reminded them how "devoutly and justly and blamelessly" they had behaved, and how they exhorted, and comforted, and charged each believer to walk worthy of God who had called them into His own kingdom and glory (1 Thessalonians 2:9-12).

Paul's statement indicates that Silas was *diligent* in all he did. In his ministry he gave himself unstintingly to exhorting and encouraging each new believer, and his self-sacrifice, coupled with the use of his gifts, helped to ground the new converts in the truth.

The Faithful Envoy

The first mention of Silas is before the second missionary journey (15:22). Certain leaders of the Jerusalem church had visited Antioch and spread false (legalistic) views of salvation (15:1-5). The matter had been referred to the apostles and elders in Jerusalem (15:6-18), and their decree was then communicated to the church in Antioch in a letter delivered by Silas (15:19-35).

But why did the Jerusalem Council select him to carry their communique to Antioch? Silas was thoroughly familiar with Greek culture and, as Dr. J. W. McGarvey has pointed out, he had been connected with work among the Gentiles. Their choice of Silas, therefore, would tend to silence any objections which legalistic Jews might have. And because Silas was a Jew and had labored in Jerusalem, he could explain to those in Antioch anything in the written document that might be obscure to them.[41]

After delivering the letter from the Jerusalem Council, Silas stayed on in Antioch encouraging and strengthening the believers (15:33) before returning to Jerusalem.

The Faithful Colleague

The unfortunate contention that caused Paul and Barnabas to go their separate ways resulted in Paul's selection of Silas as his coworker (15:40). But what led Silas to return to

---

41. J. W. McGarvey, *New Commentary on the Acts of the Apostles*, 2 vols. (Cincinnati: Standard, 1892), 2:69.

Antioch? We don't know. Paul, having seen his zeal for the Lord during his first visit to Antioch could have written to Silas requesting him to return and join him on his next missionary journey. Whatever led Silas to return, the church in Antioch approved of Paul's choice of him and committed them to the grace of God (15:40). Paul and Silas then left Antioch, traveled through Syria and Cilicia strengthening the churches, and came eventually to Derbe and Lystra.

Silas had the rare attribute of being a good follower and faithful companion of the Apostle Paul, and his presence must have been an enormous relief when embarrassing enquiries were made about the absence of Barnabas. In addition, his deliberate self-effacement made Paul's task much easier. Herbert Seekings comments on the first phase of this missionary journey:

> The rapid movements of Acts 15:40–16:12 make it impossible for the reader to grasp the greatness of this undertaking unless the places mentioned are closely followed by the aid of a map. That tour through Asia Minor which is dismissed in a verse or two was no easy matter. What patience and endurance and devotion to the will of God are hinted at in the swiftly moving record![42]

And the house-churches in which Paul and Silas ministered were edified and strengthened in the faith. We are not surprised to read, therefore, that they increased in number daily (16:4-5).

---

42. Seekings, *Men of the Pauline Circle*, 78.

At last Paul and Silas came to Philippi where Paul healed a young slave-girl who had a "spirit of divination." She brought her owners great profit by being able to predict the future (16:16). Paul mercifully released her from satanic oppression, and this immediately brought down on their heads the wrath of the girl's owners who dragged the missionaries before the magistrates. Once in the public square they were falsely accused and then unceremoniously stripped of their clothing and beaten with rods (16:22-23). After this they were thrown into the inner cell of the prison and their feet were fastened in stocks.

It is under conditions such as these that a person's faith and trust in God is tested. Several years ago I had the privilege of meeting with Hayden W. Melsop, a missionary with what was then the China Inland Mission. He was on furlough and ministering to believers in a small seaside town. We went swimming one day, and as we changed in a public change room I happened to notice the scars on his back. Without the slightest note of self-pity he told me of two occasions when he had been imprisoned in China for preaching the Gospel. His captors hoped that by subjecting him to such torture he might be induced to stop his preaching and renounce his faith in Christ.

It is while enduring such suffering that the strength of a person's courage and the reality of his/her faith is tested. Paul and Silas had reason to complain, but instead of bemoaning their fate they counted themselves privileged to suffer for Christ. They began singing psalms and hymns with the result that no one in the jail was able to sleep. Then, about midnight, the place was shaken by a great earthquake.

The doors of each cell swung open and each prisoner's chains fell off.

The next day the magistrates learned that the men they had beaten so severely were Roman citizens, and they personally came to release them. After visiting with the believers Paul and Silas journeyed on to Thessalonica. Trouble followed them, and the new converts sent them to Berea (17:10-12). As soon as Jews from Thessalonica learned of the work being done in Berea, they went there and stirred up the populace (17:13). On this occasion the Christians escorted Paul to Athens, but Silas was left to carry on the work.

This was the first time during the missionary journey that Silas had left Paul's side. He, however, stepped into the position of leadership and under his guidance the young church grew.

The brethren who conducted Paul to Athens returned with the request that Silas join Paul as soon as possible (17:15). This he did during Paul's ministry in Corinth (18:5).

Later on, Paul sent a letter to the church at Thessalonica in which he linked Silas' name with his own. It was a gracious gesture implying equality in the work of the Lord. Though they differed in gifts and temperament, each had a vital role to play in establishing the local church.

After Paul left Corinth for Antioch-on-the-Orontes, Silas possibly returned to Jerusalem. He must have continued to minister there until he joined Peter in his journeys (1 Peter 1:1).

Peter's Postscript

About thirteen years later Peter wrote to those among whom he and Silas had ministered. The letter was penned by Silas[43] whom the Apostle Peter regarded as a "faithful brother" (1 Peter 5:12).

REFLECTIONS ON A LIFE WELL-SPENT

In our church in Illinois there was a young man named Justin. He was in his late teens and had recently attended a Billy Graham Crusade. He returned overflowing with enthusiasm, and lost no time telling me that he wanted to be like Billy Graham. He wanted to drop out of school and have the church support him as he began to conduct evangelistic meetings.

I did not want to discourage Justin, but told him that Billy Graham believed in a good education. He had finished

---

43. For which NT scholars are supremely grateful. Peter was not a learned man, whereas Silas was fluent in both Greek and Hebrew. Silas was not with Peter when the apostle wrote his second letter, and the Greek text of this communique is extremely difficult to read.

high school and gone on to College, and I encouraged Justin to do the same. In the meantime he could spend time studying his Bible, preparing short messages, and praying for the Lord to lead him.

Justin did finish high school and go on to college–not because I had suggested it, but because his parents insisted on it. The last I heard of him was that he had married a girl who was not a Christian, and joined a firm in New York which had a seat on the stock exchange.

Silas was a capable and dependable worker. He had the difficult task of helping both Paul and Peter whose dominating personalities overshadowed him. Yet he possessed the qualities of faithfulness and perseverance that made him the ideal assistant of his more gifted colleagues. He was willing to take the second place, and willingly effaced himself in the service of the Lord.

When Paul wrote the believers in Rome he passed on this counsel:

> For through the grace given to me I say to everyone among you not to think more highly of himself than he ought to think; but to think so as to have sound judgment, as God has allotted to each a measure of faith. For just as we have many members in one body and all the members do not have the same function, so we, who are many, are one body in Christ, and individually members one of another. Since we have gifts that differ according to the grace given to us, each of us is to exercise them accordingly: if prophecy, according to the proportion of his faith; if service, in his serving; or he who teaches, in

his teaching; or he who exhorts, in his exhortation; he who gives, with liberality; he who leads, with diligence; he who shows mercy, with cheerfulness. Let love be without hypocrisy. Abhor what is evil; cling to what is good. Be devoted to one another in brotherly love; give preference to one another in honor; not lagging behind in diligence, fervent in spirit, serving the Lord; rejoicing in hope, persevering in tribulation, devoted to prayer, contributing to the needs of the saints, practicing hospitality. Bless those who persecute you; bless and do not curse. Rejoice with those who rejoice, and weep with those who weep. Be of the same mind toward one another; do not be haughty in mind, but associate with the lowly. Do not be wise in your own estimation (Romans 12:3-16).

We do not know if Paul had Silas in mind when he penned these words, but even if he didn't they are most appropriate, and can be taken to heart by all who would follow the Lord Jesus Christ.

CHAPTER FIVE

LUKE, PAUL'S BELOVED FRIEND

Peter Falk is remembered for his many films, and in particular his deft portrayal of the Los Angeles homicide detective, Lieutenant Colombo. In each episode of *Columbo* a murder had taken place with the perpetrator carefully concealing the crime. After the crime scene had been discovered and a wrong diagnosis of the cause of death reached by the initial investigators, Colombo would drive up in his antiquated Peugeot and, wearing a dowdy, crumpled raincoat, note some facts that did not fit the conclusion reached by the other members of the police force. Then, in his inimitable way, he would begin to piece together minute facts that eventually exposed the murderer.

While not possessing Lt. Colombo's keen powers of observation, we face a similar task when it comes to a study of Luke.[44] The celebrated biographer, Herbert Seekings, who pastored a church in Harrogate, England, wrote:

> Among the great men of the New Testament [Luke] is one of the greatest, and the most accidental mention of his name provokes thoughts of his peerless contribution

---

44. In recent years liberal scholars have disputed the authorship of Luke's gospel and the book of Acts. To avoid unnecessary controversy we shall assume that both these books were written by Luke (see Luke 1:1-4; see Acts 1:1-4). See also Acts 16:10-18; 20:5-21:18; 27:1-28:16; Colossians 4:14; Philemon 1:24; and 2 Timothy 4:20-11.

to our sacred literature. Let his share be taken from the New Testament, and it (i.e., the New Testament) would be a greatly impoverished book. [Luke] will always live in the esteem of the Church because he has given us the Third Gospel and the Acts.[45]

As we attempt to disperse the mists that obscure Luke, we catch a glimpse of a man who was both humble and gifted, devout and possessing a servant's heart, loyal and in every way a godly man. And as we piece together information about him we see him as (1) a historian, (2) Paul's physician, and (3) Paul's loyal friend.

Luke the Historian

Luke wrote his gospel and the book of Acts to place before his friend Theophilus the truth about the Lord Jesus and the work done by His disciples following His ascent into heaven. In his first treatise he desired to present facts about Jesus in a most convincing way; and in the sequel he wanted to describe the progress of the Christian church.

Theophilus was the recipient of both manuscripts. Initially he may have been a high-ranking official, and that is why Luke addressed him initially as "Most Excellent Theophilus" (Luke 1:3). When the introduction to the book of Luke is compared with the opening verses of Acts, the title is missing, and from this many Bible scholars have concluded that Theophilus had become a Christian, and on

---

45. Seekings, *Men of the Pauline Circle*, 23.

account of his stand for Christ he had been deprived of his government position.

But who was Luke? Where was he from? There are many who identify him with Lucius of Cyrene, a city in North Africa, who had taken up residence in Syrian Antioch (13:1).[46] This is most unlikely, for as Dr. John Stott has pointed out, "the conjecture of some early church fathers that Luke was referring to himself is extremely improbable, since he carefully preserves his anonymity throughout the book."[47] In reality we know nothing of Luke apart from the few clues that we can piece together from his writings.

When Paul was imprisoned for two years in Caesarea, Luke had ample time to travel about Galilee and Judea, interview eyewitnesses, and gather data for his first book. He also had the opportunity to speak directly with Mary, the mother of Jesus, and learn from her the truth about her virginal conception, the events surrounding her visit to Zacharias and Elizabeth, and learn first hand of the events of her Son's birth in a stable followed by the sequential visits of the shepherds and the Magi.

---

46. F. F. Bruce, *New Testament History*, 2d ed. (Nashville: Nelson, 1969), 289. Others hold to a similar position, claiming that Luke was a Hellenistic Jew (cf. W. F. Albright, *History, Archaeology and Christian Humanism*, 296; W. F. Arndt, *The Gospel According to St. Luke*, 2-3; and Bo Reicke, *The Gospel of Luke*, 21-22). Such a view cannot be maintained when we note how carefully Paul himself distinguished between Jewish and Gentile believers (see Colossians 4:10-14).

47. Stott, *The Spirit, the Church and the World*, 218.

Luke's research also enabled him to include in his book the *Magnificat* (Luke 1:46-55), the *Benedictus* (Luke 1:68-79), the *Gloria in Excelsus* (Luke 2:14), and the *Nunc Dimittis* (Luke 2:29-32) that have found their way into the liturgies of different churches.

A careful reading of Luke's gospel reveals some interesting facts. All four gospels quote from Isaiah 40:3-5, but only Luke includes verse 5 where we read that "all flesh shall see the salvation of God" (Luke 4:4-6). Luke also records Simeon's declaration that the life and ministry of Jesus would be "a light for revelation to the Gentiles"(Luke 2:32), and he also makes it clear that the Kingdom of God is open to all: to Samaritan and Gentile and Jew; to publicans and sinners and outcasts (Luke 24:47).

Luke's gospel contains an impressive amount of material not found in any of the other gospels. Six of the twenty miracles performed by the Lord Jesus are unique to Luke, while nineteen of the thirty-five parables in his gospel are not found in the others. And two blocks of material are peculiar to Luke (cf. 6:20–8:3 and 9:51–18:14) and contain some of the richest truths about the gospel.

Luke also manifests an interest in people, and describes how the Lord Jesus was often moved with compassion because of their suffering. He is the only writer to mention Zacchaeus, the tax collector of Jericho, and the journey of Cleopas and his companion to Emmaus. Women feature prominently in his record (Luke 2:36-38) and include Christ's raising to life the son of the widow of Nain (Luke 7:11-18), and the repentance of the sinful woman in the house of Simon the Pharisee (Luke 7:36-50). And he also mentions the role of the women who ministered to the Lord Jesus, sustaining Him and His disciples in their ministry.

It is probable that Luke, having finished his research, wrote his gospel from Caesarea.

When we turn to the book of Acts we note that Luke was an observer of certain events that took place in the history of the early Church.[48] These, as we have found, are largely identified by the "we" sections (cf. 16:10-40; 20:5-21:25, and 27:2-28:16). For the other material found in the book of Acts Luke used the accounts of eyewitnesses (e.g., the stoning of Stephen [7:54-8:1], Paul's conversion [9:1-18], the Jerusalem council [15:1-35], and much more). Place names, geographic details, and official names and titles, are abundant. Sir William Ramsay, who researched the whole area of what was formerly Asia Minor (and is now modern Turkey) came to realize that Luke was unfailingly accurate in his statements.[49]

In his writings Luke preserved the color and character of widely different people. And his record of sea voyages, of

---

48. See A. H. McNeille, *An Introduction to the Study of the New Testament*, 2d ed., rev. by C. S. C. Williams (Oxford: Clarendon, 1953), 103-110.

49. He wrote, "Every person is found just where he ought to be: proconsuls in senatorial provinces, asiarchs in Ephesus, strategoi in Philippi, politarchs in Thessalonica, magicians and soothsayers everywhere." See *The Bearing of Recent Discovery on the Trustworthiness of the New Testament*, 2d ed. (London: Hodder & Stoughton, 1915), 96-97.

hospitality shown by different people, and discussions with people of dissimilar cultures bears the mark of an authentic observer of the events.[50]

It is likely that Luke penned the Book of Acts during Paul's first imprisonment in Rome.

Luke the Physician

In addition to being a careful historian, Luke was a physician and personally attended Paul who was afflicted with "a thorn in the flesh" (cf. Colossians 4:14). As soon as we hear that Luke was a first century M.D. we tend to minimize his skills and think of him as one step above a witch doctor. Such a view, however, betrays our ignorance. As we research the history of medicine we find that certain cultures had developed the art of healing into a science. Medicine, however, came into its own between the sixth century B.C., and A.D. 200. It then entered it's own "dark ages," and it was not until the nineteenth century that it *began* to achieve any respectability.

In Egypt medicine had flowered *before* the era of Imhotep (c. 2700 B.C.), with medical texts being largely a potpourri of home remedies.[51] But from Imhotep onwards

---

50. J. Smith, *The Voyage and Shipwreck of St. Paul with Dissertations on the Life and Writings of St. Luke, and the Ships and Navigation of the Ancients*, 4th ed., rev. and corrected by W. E. Smith (Minneapolis: James, n.d.), 293pp.

advances were made in the study of anatomy as a result of surgery and embalming.[52]

In Mesopotamia the approach to medicine was not as advanced, but was no less interesting. The renowned surgeon from Johns Hopkins University, Sir William Osler, authored *Assyrian and Babylonian Medicine,* and N. Demand authored *Medicine in Ancient Mesopotamia.* They described for us the treatment of different sicknesses and diseases and it is also interesting to note the penalties for medical malpractice contained in *The Code of Hammurabi.*[53]

All of this confirms that ancient medicine had a long history and reached its peak around the time of Luke. Dr. William K. Hobart made a study of Luke's medical terminology, and was convinced that these terms proved Luke's expertise as a physician.[54] Modern linguistic scholars, however, have shown that Dr. Hobart was a little too zealous in

---

51. E. A. Wallis Budge, *Egyptian Magic* New York: Dover, 1971), 234pp. Though Dr. Budge is now deceased, he was the curator of Egyptian antiquities at the British Museum.
52. See E. A. Wallis Budge, *The Mummy,* 2d ed. (New York: Biblo & Tannen, 1964), 404pp. Several years ago, while visiting the British Museum, I was shown an example of Egyptian brain surgery. Three holes had been bored in a skull in the form of a triangle and the bone between these holes had been cut so that the portion of the skull could be removed.
53. C. Edwards, *The Hammurabi Code* (Port Washington, NY: Kennikat, 1971), items 206, 215-225.
54. W. K. Hobart, *The Medical Language of St. Luke* (Grand Rapids: Baker, 1954), 305pp.

presenting his material and tended to exaggerate some of his claims.

Of interest to us is Luke's record of Paul's healing ministry on the island of Malta. The father of Publius, the local official, was ill. Paul prayed for him, laid his hands on him, and healed him (28:8). As news of this event spread across the island people brought their sick to Paul, and they were cured (28:9). An interesting distinction is drawn between Paul's healing of the official's father, where Luke uses the word *iaomai*, "to heal," and the curing of many on the island who had diseases, where he uses the word *therapeuo*.[55] Some conjecture that Luke participated with Paul in the healing of the crowds. As evidence of this they point to 28:10 where we read that "they also honored *us* with many marks of respect."

Paul was incarcerated in Rome following his appeal to Caesar. While the Romans waited for the Jews in Judea to bring charges against him (28:30-31), he continued to minister to all who came to see him. When after about eighteen months no one came to accuse him, he was released. During this time Luke probably continued to attend to Paul's needs, and give him both material and emotional support. It is probable that the book of Acts was written during this period.

---

55. Therapeuo is "to care for, wait upon, heal, treat (medically) ...." Cf. W. Bauer's A Greek-English Lexicon of the New Testament, trans. and adapted from the 4th ed. by W. Arndt and F. W. Gingrich (Chicago: University of Chicago Press, 1979), 359.

Luke, Paul's Loyal Friend

Paul had many friends, and he mentioned them in his letters. It is significant that, when Paul sent greetings to different people, he twice listed Luke and Demas. These letters were written while Paul was in Rome, and both Luke and Demas were actively engaged in ministry in that city (Colossians 4:14; Philemon 1:23-24; and 2 Timothy 4:10). During Paul's second imprisonment, when he wrote to Timothy, he recorded with sorrow that Demas had "deserted" him. The Greek word *egkatelipen* (aorist indicative active of *egkayaleipo*, "forsook, abandoned") implies wilful departure.

In Paul's second letter to Timothy (4:9-10a) there is evidence of Paul's need for close companionship, and his emotional needs parallel our own. As Paul speaks out of the solitude of the dungeon in which he and others were confined, he remarks dejectedly that only Luke is with him (2 Timothy 4:11).[56]

Herbert Seekings sums up Paul's situation and how precious faithful friends are:

> In the day of our severest reverses few things possess for us a more heartening quality, or shed a more gracious and protecting influence over us, than devoted companionship. How often has it happened that great souls have wrested success from the grip of an apparent failure,

---

56. The Mamertine Prison in Rome is the traditional place of Paul's imprisonment.

during the face of an otherwise forlorn hope by the unyielding companionship of some comparatively unknown friend! And even when success has been out of the question the value of that rare fellowship has not been one whit the less.[57]

It is a fine tribute to Luke, the beloved physician, that he remained by Paul's side when the winds and waves of adversity threatened to overwhelm him. Whether as a historian, physician, or friend, Luke illustrates the best that human beings have to offer.

---

57. Seekings, *Men of the Pauline Circle*, 183.

CHAPTER SIX

LYDIA

Anthony Deane, in his *New Testament Studies,* calls attention to the fact that Luke, in his "travel-diary" used brief character studies or thumbnail portraits to describe the men and women whom Paul and his party met in the course of their evangelistic work. These sketches are vivid, and when considered carefully provide a convincing picture of the individuals who form a part of the narrative. The story of Lydia is a case in point.[58]

This part of Luke's story begins in Troas. After Paul had his vision of a man from Macedonia pleading with him to come and help his people, Paul and his companions put out to sea. Luke's report implies that the wind was at their backs and they were able to sail straight to Neapolis – a distance of about 156 nautical miles. The journey took only two days (whereas the return voyage took five days, 20:6).

---

58. Acts 16:13-15, 40. Lydia was from Thyatira in the province of what is today Turkey. The district in which Thyatira was situated had previously been in the ancient kingdom of Lydia, and there are many who believe that the Lydia of Acts 16 took her name from this area (in much the same way as people in the old West were called "Tex" or "Colorado," etc.). Lydia was a very common name in NT times (see Horace, *Odes,* 1:8; 3:9), and there is no reason to read into Scripture anything that isn't there (16:14).

On their way to Neapolis they spent the night sheltering in the harbor of Samothrace, protected by the 5,500 foot cliffs of Mt. Fengari Poseidon. It was on this island that the Greeks had erected the famous statue of Nike, the Winged Victory. However, when the goddess Nike failed to protect the people from the Persians, her statue was toppled over and smashed. It lay in ruins until its pieces were discovered in 1863. Her statue has now been pieced together (though the head is missing) and stands in The Louve, Paris.

The journey to the seaport of Neapolis was completed without mishap, and from there Paul and his party journeyed on foot to the ancient town of Philippi. It had been rebuilt in 356 B.C. by Philip II of Macedonia who called it after himself. With the expansion of the Roman Empire Philippi became a Roman possession in 167 B.C. Its claim to fame came in 42 B.C. when the army of Mark Anthony and Octavian defeated the army of Brutus and Cassius in a decisive battle. This victory paved the way for Octavian (who was given the name Augustus) to become emperor.

Later, the Emperor Augustus made Philippi a Roman colony–a little bit of Rome planted in a foreign land.[59] These Roman colonies were important geographic centers, and Roman veterans who had completed their military service were settled in these cities. The colonists wore Roman dress, spoke Latin, and enforced Roman laws. And nowhere was there greater pride in Roman citizenship than in these outposts of the empire.

---

59. See Harrison, ed., *Major Cities of the Biblical World*, 198-207.

Our story, however, concerns a woman named Lydia, and it is interesting to note that the "man" whom Paul saw in his vision turned out to be a woman. Everything we read about her enhances our appreciation of her.

Lydia's Occupation

When Luke spoke of Lydia's house he used the word *oikos* ("household") that often implies a family and children (cf. 1 Timothy 3:4-5, 12; 5:4). This leads us to conclude that Lydia was married and quite possibly had children. With her husband she probably belonged to a guild of dyers, and engaged in a very lucrative trade that involved the selling of very expensive purple cloth made from a dye extracted from the *Murex truneulus* shellfish. Clothing dipped in this dye was very expensive, and it was in great demand throughout the empire.

Each trade had its guild, and Sir William Ramsay tells us that there were more trade-guilds in Thyatira than in any other Asian city.[60] Each guild had its patron deity, and membership in these guilds required the worship of the patron god. Such worship was accompanied by feasting that soon degenerated into drunken orgies. Dr. John Stott is of the opinion that Lydia's habit of meeting for prayer on the bank of a river on the Sabbath indicates that she had been drawn to the higher standard of morality practiced by the Jews, though there is no evidence that she became a proselyte.[61]

---

60. W. M. Ramsay, *Letters to the Seven Churches of Asia* (New York: Armstrong, 1904), 324-25.

Wishing to be free from the debasing practices of their guild, Lydia and her family moved to Philippi where they served as the Macedonian agents of Thyatiran manufacturers. How long they lived in Philippi before the arrival of the missionaries has not been told us. Because there is no mention of Lydia's husband in Acts 16 we presume that he may have died.

Lydia's Conversion

When Paul and his party arrived in Philippi they spent several days in the city without finding a synagogue. In Jewish lore, wherever there were ten men, they could found a synagogue. On the Sabbath, therefore, the missionaries went out of the city to the small river Gangites that flowed nearby. There they found a group of women engaged in prayer and worship. They sat down and waited to be asked to speak.

One of these women was Lydia. As Paul shared with the group the message of Christ's death and resurrection, the Lord opened Lydia's heart and she believed what Paul said. Dr. Stott writes: "Although the message was Paul's, the saving initiative was God's. Paul's preaching was not effective in itself; the Lord worked through it. And the Lord's work was not in itself direct; He chose to work through Paul's preaching."[62]

---

61. Stott, *The Spirit, the Church, and the World*, 263.
62. Stott, *The Spirit, the Church, and the World*, 263.

We live in an age when "bigger" is presumed to be "better." This contrast between this attitude and the little assembly by the river side is striking. To the world those who met for prayer and worship were insignificant and unobtrusive. The people in the city went about their business and did not miss those who had gathered by the river. Other women came in from the country bringing farm products for sale or else buying food for their families, shopkeepers were busy selling their merchandise, and those responsible for administering justice were to be found sitting on a raised dias hearing complaints and trying cases.

The women who met by the river were devout (though without a knowledge of salvation through Christ) and sought to practice their beliefs in spite of the fact that the city was largely given over to pagan practices. Lydia, however, was the first to accept the Lord Jesus as her Savior. There must have been an interval of time between her conversion and her baptism, for Luke tells us that she was baptized and her household. We conclude from this that she must have gone home and told her children and any servants who lived in her house how she had come to experience salvation through Christ; and they believed and were saved.

The same is true in some homes today, but in many across the land children follow the desires of their own heart and are soon swept up in the ways of the world. This is tragic, for the Christian life in the church is based on the Christian in the family. Our homes are the mainspring of that machinery which benefits society, and the spiritual lapse that we see all about us does not bode well for society's future.

Lydia's Hospitality

As soon as Lydia had been baptized with her family she invited Paul and his associates to accept the hospitality of her home. She must have had a home that was large enough to accommodate four extra houseguests. When Lydia made her initial invitation, Paul declined. But Lydia insisted. Luke writes that she "constrained" them. The Greek *parekalesen* implies very strong persuasion. On the one hand Paul, of course, was reluctant to place himself under obligation to his converts, and on the other he did not want to expose himself to the charge of having ulterior motives. His eventual acceptance of Lydia's hospitality was unusual, but when her entreaties became so persistent he did not feel it right to continue to refuse her.

Lydia's hospitality did not slacken after the novelty of having missionaries in her home wore off. Paul and his companions stayed with Lydia for many days (16:18), and her faithfulness to the Lord was proved by her continued hospitality.

In the course of time the little church must have moved into Lydia's home, for after Paul and Silas had been released from incarceration they went to Lydia's home, and when they had seen the brethren, they encouraged them and departed for Thessalonica (16:40). And among the converts were men. It seems likely that the husbands of the women who met by the river were now believers.

ABIDING PRINCIPLES

In recent years much of our time has been spent debating the role of women in the church. These discussions have generated more heat than light. It seems that a consideration of Lydia's life frees women from such controversy.

We note that Lydia was a successful businesswoman. She is the New Testament counterpart of the woman described for us in Proverbs 31:10-31. She was a good administrator, able to handle financial matters, possibly skilled in negotiation, and at the same time a good mother who could effectively nurture her children.

Lydia was also devout. She lived up to the light she had received, and when God opened her heart to the truth, she accepted it and shared it with others.

Such was Lydia's warm response to Christ's servants that she opened her home to them. And after they had gone to other cities, the Philippian church continued to support Paul in his ministry (Philippians 4:15-17).

Because Lydia is not mentioned by name in Paul's letter to the believers at Philippi (cf. Philippians 4:1-2)[63] some have concluded that she had died. This is certainly possible. On the other hand, she may have gone back to Thyatira to spread the gospel among the dyers in that city. Whatever the

---

63. Some writers believe that Paul's true yokefellow" (Phil. 4:3) is a reference to Lydia. This is an ingenious suggestion, but it is ruled out because the adjective "true" is masculine, not feminine.

reason, Lydia's generous hospitality caused the church to emulate her example.

CHAPTER SEVEN

SONGS IN THE NIGHT

The work of evangelization in Europe had been progressing favorably. People were placing their trust in Christ for their salvation, and the opposition from the hostile Jews that Paul and his associates had encountered in Asia had been left behind. For a brief period the missionaries were enjoying the blessings of the ministry without any of its trials.

All of this was about to change.

Disruption of the Work, 16:16-18

Luke describes the disruption of the work with great accuracy.

> And it came to pass, as we were going to the place of prayer, that a certain young woman having a spirit of divination met us, who brought her masters much gain by her fortune-telling. She followed after Paul and us crying out, "These men are servants of the Most High God, who proclaim unto you the way of salvation." And this she did for many days. But Paul, becoming deeply disturbed, turned and said to the spirit, I charge you in the name of Jesus Christ to come out of her. And it came out that moment.

Paul and his companions were going to the place of prayer when they were accosted by a slave girl who had a spirit by which she was able to predict the future. Pagans throughout the ancient Near East presumed that a person with such a "gift" was possessed of a "spirit of python."[64]

This slave girl brought her owners considerable wealth by being able to predict the success or failure of business ventures, whether or not a person would marry the object of his/her heart's desire, if someone who was ill would recover, where to look for something that was lost, and a host of other concerns.

Luke does not deal with these superstitious beliefs, but goes to the heart of the matter, namely, that the young girl was possessed by an evil spirit.

At first we are inclined to think that this young girl confirmed the message that Paul and his colleagues were preaching. Those who heard her, however, were most likely pagans and would conclude that her reference to the "Most High God" was a reference to Zeus.

---

64. Python in Greek mythology was a huge female dragon or snake, born from the mud of the Flood, that guarded the cave and chasm at Delphi. Python was killed by Apollo who then took its powers becoming the motivating power of the oracle at Delphi. See the excellent discussion by M. F. Unger in *Biblical Demonology* (Wheaton, IL: Scripture Press, 1963), 140-42.

All of this raises certain the questions, Why did Paul become exasperated[65] when she continued to follow him and his party day after day?

It seems likely that Paul became dismayed by her inappropriate and unwelcome publicity because her words confused those who heard her, making it difficult for them to distinguish their pagan beliefs from Paul's presentation of the Gospel. When Paul could no longer endure her intrusion, he turned and speaking directly to the demon commanded it in the name of Jesus Christ to come out of her. And it did so.

Opposition to the Work, 16:19-24

The reaction of the young girl's owners was one of intense anger. When they found that she could no longer function as a medium they sought out Paul and Silas. Luke writes:

> But when her masters saw that the hope of their gain was gone, they laid hold of Paul and Silas, and dragged them into the marketplace before the rulers, and when they had brought them to the magistrates, they said, "These men, being Jews, do exceedingly trouble our city, and set forth customs which it is not lawful for us to receive, or to observe, being Romans." And the multitude rose up together against them: and the magistrates rent their garments, and commanded that they be beaten

---

65. The word used is *diaponeomai*, meaning "deeply disturbed."

with rods. And when they had laid many stripes upon them, they cast them into prison, charging the jailor to keep them securely. And he, having received such a charge, cast them into the inner prison, and made their feet fast in the stocks.

There is an interesting play on words in verse 19. When the slave owners realized that the evil spirit that spoke through the slave-girl was gone (*exelthen*), and that their hope of making money was also gone (*exelthen*), they dragged Paul and Silas before the magistrates. To paraphrase Luke's thought: When Paul exorcized the evil spirit from her, he exorcized their source of income as well. The charge of the slave owners was two-fold: "These men are Jews who disturb our city and introduce customs that we, as Romans, are not allowed to accept or practice."

The last thing these magistrates wanted was for a report of a disturbance within the city to reach Rome, and for disaffected citizens to claim that their leaders were permitting the propagation of beliefs that were contrary to those sanctioned by the state.[66]

---

66. Sherwin-White, *Roman Society and Roman Law in the New Testament*, 79. See also Horace, *Satires* (1:5, 34) where he shows that the Roman government regarded such actions as treasonous. The Authorized (King James) version is misleading and has led some to conclude that the magistrates tore their own clothes (16:22b). It is preferable to conclude that the magistrates ordered the *lictors* who stood by to keep law and order to remove the apostles' clothes.

So successful were the owners of the slave girl in presenting their case that the missionaries were condemned without a trial. The magistrates handed Paul and Silas over to the lictors to be flogged. This was probably the first flogging Paul received at the hands of Gentiles (cf. 2 Corinthians 11:23, 25), and one in which Silas had an equal part. The magistrates then gave them into the hands of the jailer who threw them into the dark, filthy inner cell where there was no light and no sanitation. And to add insult to injury he placed their feet in stocks. They were then left to spend the night in great pain and discomfort.

The Continuation of the Word, 16:25-39

Luke and Timothy were not included in this terrible miscarriage of justice, possibly because they did not have a prominent part in the preaching of the Gospel. Luke, however, continues the story:

> But about midnight Paul and Silas were praying and singing hymns unto God, and the prisoners were listening to them; and suddenly there was a great earthquake, so that the foundations of the prison-house were shaken: and immediately all the doors were opened, and every one's bands were loosed. And the jailer, being roused out of sleep and seeing the prison doors open, drew his sword and was about to kill himself, supposing that the prisoners had escaped. But Paul cried with a loud voice, saying, "Do thyself no harm, for we are all here."

It would be impossible to count the number of believing Christians who have been imprisoned for their faith in Christ. Some of the better known ones are John Bunyan, Adoniram Judson, William Tyndale, Richard Wurmbrand–but the list is endless.

We would not have censured Paul and Silas if they had spent their time in jail cursing the darkness, the smell, the jailer, and the judges for the injustices heaped on them. But such was not the case. They alternately prayed and sang hymns, thanking God that He had found them worthy to suffer for Christ. Among the hymns they may have sung from Israel's psalter could have been the well-known Psalm 23, "Though I walk through the valley of the shadow of death, I will fear no evil; for You are with me"; or Psalm 33, "Sing for joy in the Lord, O you righteous ones; praise is becoming to the upright"; or Psalm 34, "I will bless the Lord at all times, His praise shall continually be in my mouth"; or Psalm 37, "Do not fret because of evildoers, Be not envious toward wrongdoers, for they will wither quickly like the grass and fade like the green herb"; or Psalm 46, "God is our refuge and strength, a very present help in trouble. Therefore we will not fear, though the earth should change and though the mountains slip into the heart of the sea"; or Psalm 62, "My soul waits in silence for God only; from Him is my salvation. He only is my rock and my salvation, my stronghold; I shall not be greatly shaken," et cetera.

At midnight, while Paul and Silas were still singing their hymns of praise to God, there was a great earthquake. The prisoners, of course, could not sleep with all the singing and praying, and any who might have been dozing off would have been awakened when the earth shook so violently that the doors of their cells were opened and their chains came loose from the place where they were fastened in the wall. William Ramsay, who spent six years traveling throughout the ancient Near East as an Oxford scholar, has explained what probably happened in Philippi.

> Anyone who has seen [these] prisons will not wonder that the doors were thrown open: each door was merely closed by a bar, and the earthquake, as it passed along the ground forced the door posts apart from each other, so that the bar slipped from its hold, and the door swung open. The prisoners were fastened to the wall ... and the chains were detached from the wall, which was shaken so that spaces gaped between the stones.[67]

When the doors suddenly opened and the prisoners' chains were loosened from the wall, the question in everyone's mind is, Why didn't the prisoners escape? The answer may lie in several facts: The earthquake had been so severe that the prisoners had not fully recovered from their fears and had not yet comprehended what had happened in the dark interior of the jail.

The jailer, whose sleeping quarters were probably above the jail, came hastily to find out what had happened. He called for lights and the assistance of his *diogmitai*, "police," to help guard the prisoners. Seeing the prison doors open, he feared the worst and drew his sword to kill

---

67. Ramsay, *St Paul the Traveller and Roman Citizen*, 220-22.

himself, for he was responsible for each inmate. But Paul called out to him, "Do thyself no harm: for we are all here." Whereupon he came trembling for fear before Paul and Silas, and asked, "Sirs, what must I do to be saved?" And they said, "Believe on the Lord Jesus, and you shall be saved and your house." And they spoke the word of the Lord to him, and to all who were in his house.

The jailer had in all likelihood heard in person or learned about the slave-girl who had followed Paul and Silas calling out after them, "These men are bond-servants of the Most High God, who are proclaiming to you the way of salvation." Paul's response to the jailer's question was clear: "Believe in the Lord Jesus Christ and you shall be saved and your house" (16:31). The missionaries then "spoke the word of the Lord" to him and those in his house, explaining more fully what it meant to trust in the Lord Jesus for salvation quite apart from any works they might do.

The jailer and those in his house believed and washed Paul's and Silas' wounds, and immediately afterwards they were baptized. Then they set a meal before God's servants as an expression of their gratitude.

But this is not the end of the story.

When it was day, the magistrates sent the lictors, saying, "Let those men go." And the jailer reported these words to Paul, saying, "The magistrates have sent to let you go: now therefore depart, and go in peace." But Paul said unto them, "They have beaten us in public without trial, men who are Romans, and have cast us into prison; and now they are sending us away secretly? No indeed! But let them come themselves and bring us out." And the lictors told these words unto the magistrates: and they feared, when they heard that they were Romans. And they came and appealed to them, and when they had brought them out, they kept begging them to leave the city.

It is probable that the magistrates thought that a public flogging and a night in jail was sufficient punishment, and that the prisoners had learned their lesson. They also hoped that they would leave quietly. Paul, however, reacted differently. He claimed for himself and Silas the rights of Roman citizens, and demanded that the magistrates themselves come and escort them out of the prison.

When the magistrates heard that Paul and Silas were Roman citizens, they suffered from severe conniptions. What would happen to them if word of the previous day's activities was reported to the senate in Rome? And so the magistrates came and escorted the missionaries from prison, requesting at the same time that they leave their city.

Postscript

Before leaving Philippi Paul and Silas returned to Lydia's house in order to meet the brethren, encourage them, and say goodbye. Then they traveled along the Via Egnatia en route to Thessalonica, one hundred miles away.

Luke remained behind in Philippi and did not rejoin the missionary party until they returned to Philippi (20:5).

SOME THOUGHTS ON LUKE'S NARRATIVE

First, let us note the different types of people impacted by the Gospel. Lydia, an Asiatic, was rich and influential; the slave-girl, possibly a Greek, was from the opposite end of the social spectrum and had no property or will of her own; and the jailer, possibly a retired Roman soldier, was from the proud middle class. Each one had been reared in a different culture, yet the power of the Gospel met their deepest needs.

Second, we do not like to think of suffering as a part of the Christian life, yet the Lord Jesus told His disciples, "In the world you will have tribulation" (John 16:33), and enduring various trials aids in our maturity. Let us note that suffering is a part of the discipline of all Christ's followers (Rom 8:17; 2 Cor 1:7; Gal 3:4; Phil 3:10; 1 Thess 2:2; 2 Thess 1:5; 2 Tim 2:12; 3:12; James 5:10; 1 Peter 2:20 f; 3:14,17; 4:1,13,16; 5:10). We are called to suffer for God's or Christ's sake (Jer 15:15; Acts 9:16; Phil 1:29; 2 Tim 1:12); and this fellowship in suffering unites us with the saints of God in all times (James 5:10), and is indeed a fellowship with the Lord Himself (Phil 3:10).

Paul and Silas suffered wrongfully, and yet looked upon the experience as a furtherance of the work the Lord had given them to do.

CHAPTER EIGHT

THE HAND OF THE LORD

When I was invited to join the faculty of a graduate school my wife and I spent an evening in the home of the dean. On our arrival we found several other couples already present. After dinner, as we were all sitting in the lounge drinking coffee, our host remarked, "*I do not believe the Bible is a valid guide for life on earth.*" He then went on to state, "*In fact, I do not believe that it has the answer to any of the dilemmas mankind faces today. In my profession as a practicing psychologist I find people grappling with problems that are not discussed in the Bible. I believe that God has given us minds with which to think and reason, and He expects us to solve our own problems.*"

I was shocked by this announcement, for our host and his wife were prominent members of an evangelical church.

Of course a lively discussion ensued with the wives taking an active part. As might have been expected, the central topic focused on the prevalence of unhappy marriages in the United States. The predicaments contributing to the present malaise included the decline of the American "hero," permissiveness in the home, the virtual disappearance of the local church as a vital force in the community, and the emergence of male passivity making possible the rise of a matriarchal society.

I was the only theologian in the group, and early voiced my opinion that the better we know our Bibles, the easier it is for us to relate its teaching to a particular situation. To my dismay those present quickly set aside what I said in favor of a rationalistic approach to solving different dilemmas. The wisdom of the past was quickly dismissed in favor of modern psychological theories. The naivete of those who volunteered different approaches revealed nothing new. What they advocated had been tried before ... and failed.

The late Dr. John S. Howson wrote of the Bible:

> In no book is there so complete a code of faith and duty for all the varied circumstances of life. Broad and fearless in its statement of principles, it is also ... minute in its directions [for our] conduct. In whatever condition we may be placed, light and guidance are always provided for us in the pages of Scripture. But these statements of principles, these directions for conduct, are not always obvious on the surface, and are often supplied where we should least expect to find them. Sometimes through the indirect teaching of an example, sometimes through words dropped incidentally, and by the way; sometimes by the relation of casual circumstances, which unexpectedly reveal great truths ... we learn to "understand what the will of the Lord is" (Ephesians 5:17).[68]

As I listened to the discussion I became convinced that the story of Aquila and Priscilla offered a solution to many of the concerns being voiced by fellow faculty members and their wives. Aquila and Priscilla are mentioned six times in

---

68. Howson, *The Companions of St. Paul*, 178-79.

the New Testament, and they are always spoken of together. Apparently neither one did anything without the other,[69] and their lives led Dr. Arthur C. McGiffert to say, "They furnish the most beautiful example known to us in the apostolic age of the power for good that could be exerted by a husband and wife working in unison for the advancement of the Gospel."[70]

From Pontus to Rome

Aquila was a Jew from Pontus on the southern shores of the Black Sea. We have no means of knowing how old he was at the time he arrived in Rome, nor do we know of his profession. In keeping with Jewish tradition, however, his father had also taught him a trade.

We do not know when or under what circumstances Aquila became a Christian. In all probability it was through the influence of someone who had been to Jerusalem on the day of Pentecost (see 2:9-10). We do know that while in Rome the Lord guided him to meet and eventually marry a young, educated woman named Prisca (known affectionately by the diminutive form of her name, Priscilla). Though from different races, and different walks of life, there is every indication that their marriage was a happy one. Many Bible scholars believe that Priscilla was "high-born" (i.e., of nobility). Whether this is true or not, Dr. R. C. H. Lenski

---

69. See Acts 18:1-5, 18-21, 24-28; 1 Corinthians 16:19; Romans 16:3-5*a*; 1 Timothy 4:19.
70. A. C. McGiffert, *A History of Christianity in the Apostolic Age* (New York: Scribner's, 1916), 428.

observed, "In character, ability, and devotion she excelled her husband."[71]

In Rome, Tiberius (who had recalled Pilate from Judea) had died. He had been succeeded by Gaius Caligula, whose mad rule of only four years had plunged the once proud city into chaos. Following his assassination, Claudius was made emperor (A.D. 41). The senate had approved his appointment because they felt he would be easier to control. And all went well for about nine years. Then, in A.D. 50, the Jews caused one disturbance too many, and Claudius commanded them to leave the Imperial City (cf. 18:2*b*).[72]

From Rome to Corinth

The hand of the Lord may be seen in Claudius' command for all Jews to leave Rome, for it caused Aquila and Priscilla to leave the city on the banks of the Tiber for some other place in which to live. Though they did not know it, this move would resulted in the furtherance of the Gospel.

---

71. Lenski, *The Interpretation of the Acts of the Apostles* (1962), 768.
72. Suetonius, *Lives of the Caesars*, II:53. Suetonious wrote: "Since the Jews constantly made disturbances at the instigation of Chrestus, he expelled them from the city." Chrestus could easily be the Latinized form of Christ, and the disturbances could have been occasioned by a hostile reaction against the message of the gospel that included the teaching of Christ's resurrection.

In the decision of Aquila and Priscilla to leave Rome we see the love and devotion of this Christian couple. Priscilla, being a Roman, did not have to leave the Imperial City.[73] Some indication of the genuineness of her love for Aquila may be seen in her willingness to give up life in Rome and face with her husband an unknown future.[74]

It would have been natural for Aquila and Priscilla to experience some apprehension as they made their way to Greece. This was probably Priscilla's first trip abroad, and it would have been natural for her to be concerned about where they would live, the selection of a group of believers with whom to worship, and what kind of work would be available to Aquila? And for his part, Aquila would have been concerned about earning enough to support his wife, and how best to provide her with reasonable comforts.

---

73. See Tacitus, *Annals*, II:575, which tells how the Roman senate had ruled that a wife did not have to accompany her husband if he was sent abroad on official duty. Though this ruling was later reversed, it would have been easy for Priscilla to decide on the basis of legal precedent to remain with her family and friends while Aquila went into exile.

74. There is a great deal of information to be gleaned from J. Carcopino's book, *Daily Life in Ancient Rome*, ed. H. T. Rowell, trans. E. O. Lorimer (New Haven: Yale, 1966), 342pp. Claudius' decree meant that Priscilla would have to leave behind her family, the comfortable lifestyle to which she was accustomed, and the shops and entertainment that were a part of Roman life.

Whatever Aquila's profession may have been prior to leaving Rome, he was also a tentmaker, and he hoped that he would be able to make a living in Greece making tents. With Corinth situated on the narrow isthmus separating northern and southern Greece, and controlling trade from both East and West, this city seemed the most likely place for him to pursue his trade.

But there was another side to the wealth of cosmopolitan Corinth. It is true that the city had a reputation for commercial prosperity, but it was also known far and wide for reckless and immoral living. The famous temple of Aphrodite, the goddess of love, stood on top of the Acropolis. To this center of worship were attached one thousand priestesses who were sacred prostitutes. Each evening they would descend the hill and ply their trade in the streets of Corinth. Though the temptation was always present, Aquila never once strayed from his loyalty to Priscilla.

Aquila and Priscilla found a place in the market where they could work as tentmakers. Their shop may have had a loft above the work area where they could live. They had been in Corinth for about seven or eight months when the Lord brought to their door a weary, penniless, depressed preacher of the gospel. His name was Paul. He had a most disappointing experience in Athens and, following the rejection of his ministry there, had decided to move south to Corinth.

Aquila and Priscilla offered Paul employment, for Paul's father had also taught him the trade of tent making. And after the work of the day was done, Paul discussed the

Scriptures with them. As a result the two exiles grew in the faith.

Paul also began reasoning with the worshipers in the synagogue every Sabbath, but when Silas and Timothy came from Macedonia, Paul began devoting himself completely to the ministry of the Word, solemnly testifying to the Jews that Jesus was the Christ. When those in the synagogue resisted his ministry, he shook out his garments and said to them, "Your blood be on your own heads! I am clean. From now on I will go to the Gentiles." He then went to the house of a man named Titius Justus, a worshiper of God whose house was next to the synagogue and continued his ministry there (18:4-7).

After eighteen months, when Gallio was the proconsul of Achaia,[75] the Jews caused a disturbance and brought Paul before the judgment seat (18:12). Gallio soon discerned that the real accusation of the Jews was religious and not civil, and so dismissed the charge. After this Paul remained in Corinth "many days longer" (18:18) and then left for Syria (via Ephesus) taking Aquila and Priscilla with him.

Whereas there had been no church in Corinth prior to the arrival of the Apostle Paul, he left behind a vibrant work.

---

75. An inscription discovered at Delphi in 1905 indicates that Gallio was proconsul of Achaia in A. D. 52. This helps us date Paul's activities in Greece.

From Corinth to Ephesus

Under Paul's teaching Aquila and Priscilla had grown in their knowledge of the Scriptures, and they were now in a position to teach others. Paul left this godly couple in Ephesus, the "City of Artemis," to lay the foundation for the establishing of a new work.

Ephesus has been called the "Vanity Fair of the Ancient World," the "Supreme Metropolis of Asia," and the "Queen of Ionia." It was a particularly difficult city in which to start a work for the Lord, for the people were devout followers of Artemis (Latin, Diana) and were steeped in the black arts (cf. 19:18-20). The temple of Artemis was one of the seven wonders of the ancient world, and the Greeks had coined a phrase "the sun sees nothing finer in its course than Artemis' temple." Attached to the temple were thousands of priestesses known as *Melissae* who served the same purpose as the devotees of Aphrodite in Corinth.

Ephesus was also a "sanctuary city" and criminals from all walks of life could live in the shadow of the temple without fear of apprehension. All of this made Ephesus a difficult city in which to start a work for the Lord.

One of the most notable features in Ephesus was the famous library of Croesus. The *Ephesian Letters*–spells written in an indecipherable script – could be purchased in this library. These spells would guarantee the buyer his or her heart's desire.

The Romans had made Ephesus a "free city" granting them the right of self-government. All of this gave the Ephesians a great deal of prestige in Asia Minor (modern Turkey).

It was while Aquila and Priscilla were in Ephesus that Apollos, a Jew from Alexandria in Egypt, came to the city. He was a very learned and eloquent man and Aquila and Priscilla went to hear him. They detected that something was missing from his messages and took him aside into the privacy of their home so that they could explain to him the "way of God" with greater accuracy (18:25).

Priscilla never usurped Aquila's leadership in their home, but on the occasion of Apollos' visit Luke places her name ahead of Aquila's. It was his way of indicating that she took the initiative. Apollos had undoubtedly graduated from the leading institution(s) in Egypt, and this placed Priscilla in a position to instruct him. She was by nature more gifted than Aquila, and from all accounts he seems to have been a gentle, quiet, unobtrusive person. It is a testimony to Priscilla's tact and gracious approach that Apollos readily received her instruction, and the ministry they rendered in the privacy of their home proved to be of great benefit to the cause of Christ.

When Paul returned to Ephesus several years later he found a nucleus of believers in the city, and these went throughout Asia preaching the Word (19:10). As was Paul's custom he began ministering in the synagogue, but when the Jews rejected his words he moved to the school of Tyrannus.

This school became the center of his outreach for the next two years.

From Ephesus to Rome and Back Again

In A. D. 58 Paul again visited Corinth. He learned that Phoebe, from the church in Cenchrea, would be journeying to Rome and entrusted to her a letter that has become known as the "Letter to the Romans." Apparently the edict banishing Jews had been lifted, and Aquila and Priscilla had been allowed to returned to the proud city that had been built on seven hills. Paul was aware of this couples residence in Rome and sent them a special greeting (Roman 16:3-5*a*).

In addressing them Paul was more formal than previously, and used Priscilla's proper name, Prisca. He then added that she and Aquila were his fellow workers in Christ Jesus who had risked their lives to save his. What circumstances brought on this act of courage is not told to us, but obviously the threat was very real. Bible scholars are of the opinion that it refers to the events recorded in 19:30-31 (cf. 1 Corinthians 15:32).

Paul then went on to send greetings to the church in their house. Apparently Aquila and Priscilla were continuing to minister the Word, and had established a church in their home.

Sometime later, after Nero had become the emperor, Priscilla and Aquila felt it wise to leave Rome. They sailed for Ephesus, and apparently spent their declining years working for the Lord in that city (2 Timothy 4:19).

The effectiveness of the lives of Aquila and Priscilla may be gauged from the apostle Paul's words when he spoke of them as his "fellow-workers" whose lives had benefitted "all the churches of the Gentiles." Here we catch a glimpse of the missionary zeal of the couple.

UNIFYING THEME

The one word which seems to sum up the lives of Aquila and Priscilla is *devotion*.

First, they were devoted to one another. No circumstance of life–whether social or economic or political–separated them. Priscilla shared Aquila's spiritual aspirations and frequent hardships, and with him furthered the cause of the truth. They were the kind of couple that Alfred Tennyson called a "two-celled heart beating with one full stroke." As such they set an example for all married couples.

Second, Aquila and Priscilla, though from different social strata, did not hold their respective ethnic origins to be important. They were content that their true citizenship was in heaven, and their rightful reward would come from the Lord when they entered His presence.

Third, Aquila and Priscilla were also devoted to the truth and taught it effectively. Doing the work of evangelism in places like Ephesus or Rome was hard, and the devil did not readily yield up his territory. Yet people came to know

Christ as a result of their ministry, and in time all Asia heard the word of the Lord (19:10).

As we look about us and see the desperate need for people who seldom darken the door of a church to hear the Gospel, we are reminded of Margaret Clarkson's hymn based on Isaiah 6:8.

> So send I you to labor unrewarded, to serve unpaid, unloved, unsought, unknown,
> > To bear rebuke, to suffer scorn and scoffing—so send I you to toil for Me alone....
>
> So send I you to loneliness and longing, with heart a-hung'-ring for the loved and known,
> > Forsaking home and kindred, friend and dear one—so send I you to know My love alone.
>
> So send I you to leave your life's ambition, to die to dear desire, self-will resign,
> > To labor long and love where men revile you—so send I you to lose your life in Mine.

CHAPTER NINE

FELIX, THE UNHAPPY GOVERNOR

When Paul saw the risen Lord Jesus on the road to Damascus he was blinded by Christ's glory, and those who were with him had to lead him by the hand into the city (9:3-8). In the city, the Lord appeared to Ananias, a devout believer, and told him to go to Paul and pray for him so that he might receive his sight.

> Now there was a disciple at Damascus named Ananias; and the Lord said to him in a vision, "Ananias." And he said, "Here I am, Lord." And the Lord said to him, "Get up and go to the street called Straight, and inquire at the house of Judas for a man from Tarsus named Saul, for he is praying, and he has seen in a vision a man named Ananias come in and lay his hands on him, so that he might regain his sight .... He is a chosen instrument of Mine, to bear My name before the Gentiles and kings and the sons of Israel; *for I will show him how much he must suffer for My name's sake"* (9:10-16, emphasis added).

Ananias did as the Lord commanded him, and the rest of the book of Acts is a record of Paul's trials as he sought to carry out the mandate the Lord Jesus had given him.

Paul listed some of his sufferings in 2 Corinthians 11:24-27, but here in Acts 21:27–28:31 we have a more detailed account of the injustices which he experienced.

These began with the false accusation of Asian Jews who had come to Jerusalem for worship. Paul had been warned by believers in different places that sufferings awaited him in Jerusalem (20:22-27; 21:4*b*, 10-12),[76] and there are many writers who are quick to claim that he sinned against the Holy Spirit by ignoring the united testimony of these godly followers of Christ. These critics of the Apostle Paul do so to detract from his apostolic authority. They, however, fail to draw a distinction between *prediction* and *prohibition*. Paul did not dispute what these believers were predicting. All he did was affirm his willingness to suffer for the things he believed in. He said:

> "And now, compelled by the Spirit, I am going to Jerusalem, not knowing what will happen to me there. I only know that in every city the Holy Spirit warns me that prison and hardships are facing me. However, I consider my life worth nothing to me, if only I may finish the race and complete the task the Lord Jesus has given me--the task of testifying to the gospel of God's grace (20:22-24).

Paul's Sufferings in Jerusalem

The predictions of Paul's sufferings began to be fulfilled when, after a week in Jerusalem, he went to the Temple to pay his vow. Certain Jews from Asia saw him and

---

76. While in Caesarea Agabus predicted that Paul would be seized by the Jews and handed over to the Gentiles (21:10-11). It is significant that Philip's daughters who lived in the same city did not voice the same prediction (21:8-9).

falsely accused him of profaning the Temple and propagating false doctrine (21:27-30). These charges were untrue, but they were sufficient to arouse the people to band together to kill Paul.

Paul was saved only when the Roman commander with a cohort of soldiers came and rescued him out of their hands (21:31-33). Because the crowd was unsure of the crime(s) Paul was supposed to have committed, the commander could not ascertain the real reason for the attack on his life. He took him into the fort of Antonia (21:34), and the next day Paul was brought before the Sanhedrin (22:30–23:1).

The high priest at this time was a particularly unsavory character named Ananias. Dr. Warren W. Wiersbe writes: "Ananias was indeed one of the most corrupt men ever to be named high priest. He stole tithes from other priests and did all he could to increase his authority. He was known as a brutal man who cared more for Rome's favor than Israel's welfare."[77]

Paul began his defense before the Sanhedrin by personally recounting his early life as a Pharisee and a persecutor of "The Way." When this failed to convince those who were present of his loyalty to Judaism, he switched his defense to doctrine. He had noticed that those present were both Sadducees and Pharisees. He outlined his beliefs, and all went

---

77. All of Wiersbe's works are of the utmost value to lay Bible students. He carefully distinguishes between Ananias the high priest of Acts 23 and the high priest named Annas of Acts 4:6 (see Wiersbe's *Bible Exposition Commentary*, vol. 1 [Wheaton, IL: Victor, 1989], 494).

well until he began to speak about the resurrection (23:6). This precipitated a vehement discussion between the two groups (23:7).

The Pharisees outnumbered the Sadducees,[78] and when learned scribes said "We find nothing wrong with this man," Paul should have been released. The furor, however, continued and the commander of the garrison was afraid that Paul might be torn to pieces. To save his life he took Paul by force and brought him into the security of the Roman barracks.

But this wasn't the end of the Jews' efforts to rid themselves of Paul. So imminent was the threat against Paul's life that the Lord Jesus appeared to him in the night assuring him that he must still witness about Him in Rome (23:11).[79]

The Asian Jews had been frustrated in their attempt to lynch Paul, and the Sanhedrin had been unable to convict him of any offense, so now a group of more than forty Jews hatched a plot to murder him. They approached the Sanhedrin with the suggestion that the chief priests persuade the

---

78. The Sadducean party came from the ranks of the priests, the party of the Pharisees from the scribes. The characteristic feature of the Pharisees arises from their legalism, that of the Sadducees from their social position. Although the Sadducean high priests were at the head of the Sanhedrin, the decisive influence upon public affairs was in the hands of the Pharisees (cf. 23:8-9).

79. It is interesting to note that the Lord Jesus did not reprove Paul for going to Jerusalem.

commander to take Paul to Caesarea for trial before the governor. They would attack the party en route to the coast and kill Paul. The plan was a simple one. What could possibly go wrong?

In the providence of God, Paul's nephew[80] overheard what was being discussed and told Paul. Paul arranged for the lad to tell the commander of the plot. The fact that the commander did not hesitate to believe the boy's report tacitly indicates his belief that such a scheme was fully in keeping with the machinations of the Jews. He immediately called two centurions and instructed them to be ready at 9:00 P.M. with a company 470 armed men (made up of cavalry and infantry) to take Paul to Caesarea (23:23-24). He also wrote a letter to the Governor, Antonius Felix, in which he stated that Paul had done nothing worthy of death or imprisonment (23:29).

Luke preserves for us this copy of the letter:

Claudius Lysias, to the Most Excellent Governor Felix

---

80. We know nothing of Paul's sister or the family from which he came, except for the veiled reference in Philippians 3:8 where he intimates that he had lost his family when he became a Christian. John Pollock, in his insightful book on Paul's life entitled *The Apostle: The Life of Paul* (Wheaton, IL: Victor, 1985), states "My personal reading of the scanty evidence is that Paul was ... a widower, or, more probably, had been repudiated by his wife when he returned to Tarsus a Christian."

Greetings.

When this man was arrested by the Jews and was about to be killed by them, I came up to them with the troops and rescued him, having learned that he was a Roman. And wanting to ascertain the charge for which they were accusing him, I brought him down to their Council; and I found him to be accused over questions about their Law, but under no accusation deserving death or imprisonment. When I was informed that there would be a plot against the man, I sent him to you at once, also instructing his accusers to bring charges against him before you (23:26-30).

It is important to note in passing that this was the second time Paul had been pronounced innocent, and he should have been released without delay.

Paul's Trial in Caesarea

Felix was originally a slave who, for some unknown service or fortuitous friendship, had been freed. He achieved distinction with the legions of Rome, and Suetonius speaks of the military honors the emperor conferred upon him.[81] Claudius later appointed Felix to the governorship of Judea. Such advancement, however, did not make Felix either a happy or an honorable man. Tacitus in his *History* declares that during his governorship Felix indulged in all kinds of cruelty and lust, exercising regal power with the disposition

---

81. Suetonius, V: 28-29.

of a slave.[82] In addition, in his *Annals,*[83] he represents Felix as considering himself licensed to commit any crime, relying on the influence of those at court in Rome to protect him.

During his governorship Flix was asked to pronounce sentence on the Apostle Paul.

Once in Caesarea, Paul was kept in Herod's Praetorium for five days pending the arrival of Ananias and the elders. When they were all present their lawyer, a man named Tertullus, addressed the court. He was in all probability a Roman trained in the art of rhetoric and therefore skilled in the principles of oratory and persuasion. As a Roman he would be acceptable to Felix, and as a lawyer he was obviously someone whom the Jewish leaders could bend to their will. In discussing legal training Aristophanes, the great Athenian satirist, stated that the object of sophistic instruction (i.e., legal reasoning) was "to make the worse appear the better reason," and Tertullus was adept in such duplicity.

When Paul's accusers had arrived he was brought before the Governor.

Tertulles' opening statement shows that he was skilled in the use of flattery. He began by complimenting Felix on his reforms and the peace he had achieved. It was true that Felix had put down certain revolts, but it left unexplained why a large contingent of soldiers was needed to guard one

---

82. Tacitus, *Histories*, V: 9.
83. Tacitus, *Annals*, XII:54.

prisoner en route to Caesarea. Though Tertullus' comments were a fabrication of the truth they did create a favorable setting for the accusations to follow (24:2b-8).

Three indictments were leveled against Paul. They may be paraphrased as follows: *Personal* ("he is a troublemaker who has stirred up riots among the Jews all over the world"); *Political* ("he is the ringleader of the Nazarene sect"); and *Doctrinal* ("he has desecrated the Temple"). Of course, the Jews from Asia were Paul's prime critics, but they were not present in Caesarea.

The use of negative, slanted terms should not escape the attention of the reader (e.g. "a ringleader," "stirred up riots," "all over the world," "sect," "desecrated"). They were designed to prejudice Felix in favor of the Jewish leaders.

In a final, deft move Tertullus tried to impugn the integrity of Lysias, claiming that when the Jews in Jerusalem were attempting to judge Paul according to their law,[84] he came with soldiers and used unnecessary force to take Paul into custody.

Tertullus concluded his prosecution with a direct appeal to Felix by saying, "By examining him yourself[85] concerning all these matters you will be able to ascertain the things

---

84. I.e., lynch Paul.
85. A euphemistic expression implying the use of torture. It was common knowledge that under the most painful forms of torture a prisoner could be induced to saying anything.

of which we accuse him." The Jews also joined in, asserting that these things were so (24:8-9).

Felix then motioned for Paul to begin his defense. Paul was respectful in addressing the Governor. He refrained from the kind of loquacious flattery Tertullus had used, and his refutation of the charges was clear and concise:

"Twelve days ago I went up to Jerusalem to worship. Neither in the Temple, nor in the synagogues, nor in the city itself did they find me carrying on a discussion with anyone or causing a riot. Nor can they prove to you the charges of which they now accuse me. But this I admit to you, that according to the Way which they call a sect I do serve the God of our fathers, believing everything that is in accordance with the Law and that is written in the Prophets; having a hope in God, which these men cherish themselves, that there shall certainly be a resurrection of both the righteous and the wicked. In view of this, I also do my best to maintain always a blameless conscience both before God and before men.

"Now after several years I came to bring alms to my nation and to present offerings; in which they found me occupied in the Temple, having been purified, without any crowd or uproar. But there were some Jews from Asia--who ought to have been present before you and to make accusation, if they should have anything against me. Or else let these men themselves tell what misdeed they found when I stood before the Council, other than for this one statement which I shouted out while standing among them, 'For the resurrection of the dead I am on trial before you today'" (24:11-21).

The absence of the Asian Jews was a serious breach of Roman law.[86] But this was only one of the many breaches of Rome's legal procedure.

Felix dismissed Tertullus and the Jews. He could not convict Paul, because Lysias had found him innocent. Being on the proverbial "horns of a dilemma" he stated that he would wait for the coming of Lysias when he would decide Paul's case. Meanwhile Paul was kept under guard but given certain freedom. His friends were also permitted to see him and care for his needs.

Several days later Felix asked that Paul be brought before him. This time his wife Druscilla was with him. Druscilla was not his first wife, but his third. As the daughter of Herod Agrippa I she had been married to Azis of Emesa when she was about sixteen years of age. When Felix saw her he was so taken by her beauty that he wanted her for his wife. He sent to her a man named Simon, a Jewish Cypriot, who pretended to be a magician, to induce her to leave her husband and marry the Governor. Apparently Simon traded on her fears, while Felix promised to make her supremely happy. In the end she left her husband and mar-

---

86. Sherwin-White, *Roman Society and Roman Law in the New Testament*, 52.

ried Felix,[87] and in the course of time bore Felix a son whom she named Agrippa after her father.

This couple listened to Paul as he discoursed on righteousness, self-control and judgment to come. So powerful were Paul's words that Felix trembled. Fearing the loss of self-control he dismissed Paul with the words "When I have a more convenient time I will send for you." (Luke records that at the same time he was hoping that Paul would offer him a suitable bribe.)

After two years with no one bringing any verifiable charges against him, Paul should have been released. But when Felix was recalled to Rome he left Paul bound in order to please the Jews. He was much older than Druscilla, and inasmuch as nothing further is known about him, we are left to presume that he died. Drusilla and her son moved to the town of Campanian on the outskirts of Pompeii. When Vesuvius erupted on August 24, A.D. 79, the two of them were apparently buried beneath the volcanic ash that descended on the city. Drusilla was 39 or 40 years of age.

AN OPPORTUNITY LOST

As far as we know Felix never experienced "a more convenient time" to become a Christian. He knew the truth. His wife had firsthand knowledge of the righteous power of

---

87. Josephus, *Antiquities of the Jews*, XX: 7: 2.

God, for her father had gone to Caesarea to met with a large delegation of Jews. In the amphitheater he attacked the new movement that had sprung up around the person and teachings of Jesus Christ. He hoped thereby to placate the Pharisees and Sadducees who were enemies of the new movement (12:1-4, 19-23).

Josephus tells us that he came in dressed in glittering silver cloth. When he arrived at the theater early in the morning the sun's rays shone on his clothing. And as he spoke the crowd acclaimed him a god. He immediately experienced a severe pain in his stomach, collapsed, and soon thereafter died.[88]

All of this was known to Druscilla and Felix. They knew that the God whom Paul served was not to be trifled with. There was nonetheless a struggle in their hearts between the pleasures of the world that they wanted to enjoy, and the need to care for their spiritual well-being. They *procrastinated* ... and as far as we know died without being saved from their sins.

---

88. Josephus, *Antiquities of the Jews*, XIX: 8: 2.

CHAPTER TEN

PAUL'S APPEAL TO CAESAR

According to Josephus, Felix was recalled to Rome in order to explain his savage suppression of a dispute between Jews and Syrians over their respective civil rights in Caesarea. Tradition affirms that he would have been severely punished had it not been his brother Pallas' appeal to Nero.[89]

After Felix's recall to Rome he was succeeded by a new governor named Porcius Festus. Festus wanted to avoid the problems that had led to his predecessor's recall, and took up his duties with the intention of doing what was right. He soon discovered, however, that the Jews were not easy to handle, and that the two-year-old case of the Apostle Paul had lost none of its porcupine-like bristles. Felix faced a very delicate situation, for Paul was a Jew whose countrymen wanted to kill, and he (Festus) was a Roman whose government did not know what to do with him.[90]

Festus knew that if he released Paul, the Jews would cause trouble, as they had done for Pilate and every governor since his time. And if he held Paul a prisoner he knew he would have to explain to his superiors why a Roman citizen was being held without criminal charges being brought

---

89. Josephus, *Antiquities of the Jews*, XX: 8: 7, #9; *Wars of the Jews*, II: 13: 7.
90. Wiersbe, *Bible Exposition Commentary*, I:502.

against him. He knew, too, that the best thing he could do would be to act quickly and take advantage of the fact that he was a newcomer. To delay would only make the problem worse!

Chapters 25 and 26 deal with Festus (1) Trying diplomatic measures to resolve the issue (25:1-12); (2) Deliberating with King Agrippa during the latter's official visit to Caesarea (25:13-22), and (3) Deciding upon a course of action after listening to Paul's defense (25:23–26:32).

Festus' Visit to Jerusalem (25:1-5)

Upon arriving in Caesarea Festus acted promptly. After three days he went up to Jerusalem. There the chief priests and the leading men of the Jews brought charges against Paul. They hoped that the sheer number of charges would be sufficient to induce the Governor to place the disposition of Paul's case in their hands. To this end they were urging him, as a favor to them, to have Paul brought to Jerusalem for trial. At the same time, Luke learned that the priests had conspired with a fanatical group known as the *Sicarii* (or Assassins) to kill Paul when he was en route to Jerusalem.[91]

Though Festus has been accused of being impulsive and not thinking through the implications of his spontaneous decisions,[92] in Jerusalem he stood firm and refused to

---

91. Cf. Josephus, *Antiquities of the Jews*, XX: 8: 6, #9; *Wars of the Jews*, VII: 8: 1.
92. Cf. Seekings, *Men of the Pauline Circle*, 239-45.

have his prisoner brought before the Sanhedrin. Instead, he invited Paul's accusers to come to Caesarea where Paul would be tried before him. He invited influential men among the Jews to go there with him, and if there was any validity in their accusations, they could prosecute him.

Paul's Trial in Caesarea (25:6-12)

After spending eight or ten days in Jerusalem, Festus returned to Caesarea where he convened his court. The Jews stood around Paul and accused him of many things. Of course, an accusation could not become a valid charge unless it was supported by witnesses, and this is what the Jews lacked. The Jews also knew that Roman governors were unwilling to convict on purely religious grounds, and therefore tried to give their allegations a political twist.[93]

Finally, in an endeavor to placate the Jews, Festus asked Paul if he was prepared to go to Jerusalem to be tried there. Paul knew that to accede to this proposal would place him in a position where he could not hope for justice. His only assurance of a fair trial and possible acquittal lay with a Roman court. He, therefore, said:

> "I am standing before Caesar's tribunal, where I ought to be tried. I have done no wrong to the Jews, as you also very well know. If, then, I am a wrongdoer and have committed anything worthy of death, I do not refuse to die; but if none of those things is true of which

---

93. Sherwin-White, *Roman Society and Roman Law in the New Testament*, 50-51, 57-70.

these men accuse me, no one can hand me over to them. I appeal to Caesar."

Paul's Testimony Before Agrippa (25:13–26:32)

A few days later King Agrippa II arrived in Caesarea with his sister Queen Bernice. The intent of the visit was to pay their respects to the new governor. King Agrippa[94] was a man of singular ability with a comprehensive knowledge of Judaism. He was the son of Herod Agrippa I (see 12:1-4; 19-23), and the grandson of Herod the Great who had murdered the children of Bethlehem. It was widely believed that brother and sister were involved in an incestuous relationship. Juvenal, the Roman satirist, wrote:

That far-famed gem which Berenice wore,
The hire of incest and therefore valued more,
A brother's present, in that barbarous state
Where king's the sabbath barefoot celebrate,
And old indulgence grants a length of life
To hogs that fatten fearless of the knife.[95]

---

94. Josephus, *Antiquities of the Jews*, XX: 8: 4, #159; *Wars of the Jews*, II: 13: 2. Information about his personal life may be gleaned from Josephus, *Antiquities of the Jews*, XX: 7: 3, #145-47; Juvenal, *Satires*, VI: 156, 160; and S. Perowne, *The Later Herods* (London: Hodder & Stoughton, 1958), 189-91.

Festus was probably happy to entertain King Agrippa and Queen Bernice, and after the usual banquets he broached the subject of Paul's imprisonment.

"There is a certain man left a prisoner by Felix, about whom the chief priests and the elders of the Jews informed me, when I was in Jerusalem, asking for a judgment against him. To them I answered, 'It is not the custom of the Romans to deliver any man to destruction before the accused meets the accusers face to face, and has opportunity to answer for himself concerning the charge against him.' Therefore when they had come together, without any delay, the next day I sat on the judgment seat and commanded the man to be brought in. When the accusers stood up, they brought no accusation against him of such things as I supposed, but had some questions against him about their own religion and about a certain Jesus, who had died, whom Paul affirmed to be alive. And because I was uncertain of such questions, I

---

95. Bernice (also spelled Berenice) was the daughter of Agrippa I, and the sister of Druscilla. She was a very beautiful woman. Her first marriage was to Marcus, a Jewish official in Alexandria, Egypt. He died, and her father then betrothed her to her uncle, the king of Calchis. He, too, died, but not before giving her two sons. As a widow Bernice came to live with her brother. It was inevitable that rumors would spread of an incestuous relationship, and these persisted for the next half century. Her several marriages and other love affairs are chronicled by Juvenal, *Satires*, 155-60; and Tacitus, *Histories,* 2:81. Her brief relationship with the Emperor Titus is to be found in Suetonius, "Titus," 7:2.; and her life is summarized by Perowne, *The Later Herods*, 189-91.

asked whether he was willing to go to Jerusalem and there be judged concerning these matters. But when Paul appealed to be reserved for the decision of Augustus,[96] I commanded him to be kept till I could send him to Caesar" (25:14-21).

Intrigued by Festus' summary of the case, Agrippa expressed his desire to hear Paul. Festus lost no time in convening a meeting for the next day. Luke tells us that Agrippa and Bernice came into the hall with great pomp (24:23a). In all probability they wore their royal robes of purple and gold, and each had a small gold crown on his/her head. Not to be outdone, Festus was probably attired in the scarlet robe which governors wore on state occasions. The dignitaries most likely entered the audience room with much less ostentation. Finally, high ranking officers, military tribunes, and the leading men of the city came to be seated.

When everyone was present, Festus gave instructions for Paul to be brought in. Then, with the prisoner before them, Festus introduced the proceedings by saying:

> "King Agrippa and all the men who are here present with us, you see this man about whom the whole assembly of the Jews petitioned me, both at Jerusalem and here, crying out that he was not fit to live any longer. But when I found that he had committed nothing deserving of death, and that he himself had appealed to Augustus (i.e., the emperor), I decided to send him. I have nothing certain to write to my lord concerning him.

---

96. A title given the emperor.

Therefore I have brought him out before you, and especially before you, King Agrippa, so that after the examination has taken place I may have something to write. For it seems to me unreasonable to send a prisoner and not to specify the charges against him" (25:24-27).

Festus' preamble was not entirely accurate. It was true that the Jewish community in Jerusalem had petitioned for Paul to be put to death, but Festus had not found him guilty of any capital crime. He also erred in his statement that he did not have any specific charge against him. The charges of the Jews had been many and specific. The trouble was that there was no evidence to support them

Following this introduction, King Agrippa motioned to Paul and said, "You have permission to speak for yourself."

The scene is not difficult to visualize. Seated all around were the rich and powerful, and in the center a poorly clad prisoner in chains. In an earlier chapter we quoted from *The Acts of Paul and Thecla* where we are given a description of Christ's apostle. According to this source Paul was short, bandy-legged, balding, had bushy eyebrows, and a large hooked nose. But he was possessed of a quiet confidence that spoke of great inner strength and courage.

Paul began by acknowledging Agrippa's familiarity with Jewish customs, and then proceeded to tell his story. He described (1) His early life and training as a strict Pharisee; (2) His career as a fanatical persecutor of those who adhered to "the Way"; and (3) An account of his experience on the Damascus highway when the risen Lord Jesus appeared to him and commissioned him to preach the gospel to both Jews and Gentiles.

Early life and training as a strict Pharisee. Paul began by reminding Agrippa and all who were present that "the Jews all know the way I have lived ever since I was a child, from the beginning of my life in my own country, and also in Jerusalem. They have known me for a long time and can testify, if they are willing, that according to the strictest sect of our religion, I lived as a Pharisee. And now it is because of my hope in what God has promised our fathers that I am on trial today. This is the promise our twelve tribes are hoping to see fulfilled as they earnestly serve God day and night. O king, it is because of this hope that the Jews are accusing me. Why should any of you consider it incredible that God raises the dead?" (26:4-8).

Paul had sat at the feet of the great Rabbi Gamaliel, Israel's celebrated doctor of the law, and one of the most respected men in the land. Under Gamaliel he had gained a reputation for scholarship, righteousness, and religious zeal. There must have been many still alive who could vouch for the accuracy of his words. And being devout and law abiding it was incredulous that he should have been tried for supposed sins against the Jewish nation. The twelve tribes were eagerly awaiting the coming of the Messiah who would redeem His people. Paul affirmed that He had already come, and that His resurrection from the dead was the proof of His Messiahship.

Paul's career as a fanatical persecutor of those who adhered to the Way. Paul continued, "In my misguided zeal

I thought that I must do many things contrary to the name of Jesus of Nazareth. This I also did in Jerusalem, and many of the saints I shut up in prison, having received authority from the chief priests; and when they were put to death, I cast my vote[97] against them. And I punished them often in every synagogue and compelled them to blaspheme; and being exceedingly enraged against them, I persecuted them even to foreign cities" (26:9-11).

As a Pharisee Paul was convinced that the "sect" of the Nazarene posed a threat to Judaism, and that its adherents were guilty of heresy. He, therefore, imprisoned many, and even had others flogged in an endeavor to get these young believers to blaspheme the name of the Lord Jesus.

The faith of these Christians, even under torture, may have comprised some of the goads to which the Lord referred when He confronted Paul on the road to Damascus.

Paul's conversion on the Damascus highway. "While I was journeying to Damascus with the authority and commission of the chief priests, at midday, O King, I saw on the way a light from heaven, brighter than the sun, shining all around me and those who were journeying with me. And when we had all fallen to the ground, I heard a voice saying to me in the Hebrew dialect, 'Saul, Saul, why are you persecuting Me? It is hard for you to kick against the goads.' And I said, 'Who are You, Lord?' And the Lord said, 'I am Jesus whom you are persecuting. But get up and stand on your

---

97. The phrase "I cast my vote" or "registered my vote" suggests that Paul was a member of the Sanhedrin.

feet; for this purpose I have appeared to you, to appoint you a minister[98] and a witness not only to the things which you have seen, but also to the things in which I will appear to you; rescuing you from the Jewish people and from the Gentiles, to whom I am sending you, to open their eyes so that they may turn from darkness to light and from the dominion of Satan to God, that they may receive forgiveness of sins and an inheritance among those who have been sanctified by faith in Me'" (26:12-18).

Damascus was one of the "foreign cities" Paul determined to purge of heretics. So thorough was he in his plans to exterminate all followers of "the Way," that he had in his possession special extradition letters authorizing him to arrest all adherents to this new "sect."

When Paul was confronted by irrefutable evidence of Christ's resurrection the Lord commissioned him to be a witness to His resurrection; and His promise was that He would rescue him from his own people and from the Gentiles. Paul's message was to bear testimony to what he had seen in order that the eyes of the unbelieving Gentile world might be opened, and their ears unstopped. The promise of forgiveness of sins was part of his message. It also promised that each believer would be translated from the kingdom of darkness into the kingdom of light, or, more specifically, from the power of Satan to God.

---

98. The word usually translated "minister" (26:16) is *hyperetes*, and is used of a lowly slave (an under-rower) on a galley ship.

Paul then turned from Christ's commission of him to his response to it. He was not disobedient to the Lord's appointment of him, for the evidence of Christ's resurrection was too vivid and real to allow for any contradiction. He, therefore, began to tell others about the risen Lord Jesus in Damascus as well as elsewhere. And his message conformed to the teaching of the Old Testament prophets, for they taught that Christ, the Messiah, would suffer and die, that He would rise from the dead, and that the light of His saving grace would be proclaimed to Jews and Gentiles alike (cf. Isaiah 53:4-12; see also 42:6; 49:6; 52:14).

In a court proper decorum is maintained. Following Paul's defense the exact opposite was the case. Festus interrupted Paul and said, "You are out of your mind. Your great learning has made you mad!" In terms commonly in use today, one might attempt to refute such a strong presentation of the Gospel by stating that Christ's messenger is too fanatical for rational people to believe what he says. And those who engage in evangelism know that this happens all too often.

Paul was not to be sidetracked from his message. He had been testifying before Agrippa, and he continued to keep his focus on the king (26:27). He knew that Agrippa was familiar with the prophets, and that everything he had affirmed was to be found in the teaching of God's messengers to His people Israel.

Agrippa, however, did not like having the initiative taken away from him. He responded, "You almost persuade me to be a Christian" (26:28).[99]

His words became the basis of a hymn by Philip Bliss that was popular at one time:

> "Almost persuaded" now to believe;
> "Almost persuaded" Christ to receive:
> Seems now some soul will say,
> "Go, Spirit, go away;
> Some more convenient day
> On Thee I'll call.

When Agrippa rose to his feet he indicated that the meeting was over. Festus and Agrippa briefly discussed Paul's case and concluded that he was innocent. They went so far as to say that, had he not appealed to Caesar, he could have been set free.

The later history of King Agrippa II gives no indication that he ever turned to Christ for the salvation of his immortal soul. The last stanza of Philip Bliss' hymn summarized the experience of many who procrastinate:

> "Almost persuaded," harvest is past!
> "Almost persuaded," doom comes at last!
> "Almost" cannot avail,
> "Almost" is but to fail!
> Sad, sad the bitter wail,
> "Almost," but lost!

---

99. Some translations have "In a short time you will persuade me to become a Christian." Whether said in jest or sarcasm, Paul expressed his wish for Agrippa and all who were present to become as he was apart from his chains.

CHAPTER ELEVEN

THE VOYAGE TO ROME

The last time Paul was in Ephesus he told the believers in that city that he also wanted to visit Rome (19:21). Much had happened since then. Now, however, he was about to set sail for the City on Seven Hills. What do you think his feelings were as he boarded the first of the three ships that would take him there?

From Caesarea to Myra, 27:1-7

It is possible that his emotions were mixed. His plans to visit Rome had been hindered by interminable delays. He had expected to journey to Rome as a free citizen. Instead, he was in chains and standing in the hot sun on the quay of Caesarea, looking out over the azure blue waters of the Mediterranean. The first ship that Paul went aboard was an Adramyttian ship that took him as far as Myra in Lycia.[100]

In all there were two hundred and seventy-six people on board (27:37). The centurion into whose care Paul had been committed was a man named Julius. He appears to have been a quiet man, experienced in command.

---

100. The whole story is told in Acts 27:1–28:31. It will be helpful for readers to keep a map of the Mediterranean open before them as they study this chapter. Adramyttium was a port on the Aegean opposite Lesbos.

Accompanying Paul were Luke (note the use of "we" in 27:1) and Aristarchus (see 20:4). Perhaps Luke was taken along as Paul's physician (or, perhaps, as the ship's doctor), and Aristarchus may have been listed on the passenger manifest as either Paul's or Luke's assistant.

When all were aboard, the vessel set out to sea. Hugging the coastline, the captain made for Sidon, sixty-seven miles away. There Julius allowed Paul to visit friends and receive care. It was most unusual for a prisoner to be given freedom to visit friends, and Julius' gracious act sheds further light on his character. He was a keen judge of human nature and knew that Paul could be relied upon to return to the ship at a given time. Just what was involved in the "care" Paul received from his friends is not told us. Paul's visit with his friends possibly lasted as long as it took to take certain freight on board the ship.

On leaving Sidon, Luke, who always paid close attention to details, stated that when they put out to sea they sailed under the shelter of Cyprus.[101] The prevailing early autumn winds came from the northwest, making headway difficult for a coastal vessel. It was deemed the better part of wisdom to sail around the eastern end of Cyprus before heading north for the coast of Cilicia.

In time, after sailing past Pamphylia (where John Mark had deserted Paul on the first missionary journey) they arrived at the port of Myra on the southern end of Asia

---

101. Cf. Smith, *The Voyage and Shipwreck of St. Paul*, 61-73.

Minor (modern Turkey). Here all passengers were transferred to an Alexandrian ship carrying wheat to Italy.

At first all went well. Because of the hazzards of travel at this time of year, the shipmaster made straight for Cnidus, a port on the southwestern end of Asia Minor. The journey must have been very uncomfortable, for the ship pitched and rolled on account of the adverse winds and the heavy seas. The captain was unable to dock at Cnidus, and these offshore winds drove the heavily laden galley south. All on board were finally able to obtain a measure of relief when the captain charted a course along the leeward side of the island of Crete.

From Myra to Crete, 27:7-13

Halfway along this 140-mile island is a harbor called Fair Havens. Here Paul urged the shipmaster and the centurion to spend the winter (27:8-11).

Ignoring Paul's counsel, the shipmaster put out to sea with the intent of reaching the harbor at Phoenix. As soon as they had left the shelter of the mountains at Fair Havens a nor'easter broke on them with unprecedented fury.[102] The name given this treacherous northeasterly wind was *Euraquilo*, a hybrid word, half Greek and half Latin (from Euros, "east wind," and *Aquilo* "north wind"). James Smith includes in his *Voyages and Shipwreck of St. Paul* a few lines by William Falconer that appeared in *The Marine Dictionary*:

---

102. Smith, *The Voyage and Shipwreck of St. Paul*, 98.

> The flattering wind that late with promis'd aid
> From Candia's bay th' unwilling ship betray'd
> No longer fawns beneath the fair disguise,
> But like a ruffian on his quarry flies.

The Storm, 27:9-38

Once again the ship was driven off course. As they sailed along the leeward side of a small island named Clauda they struggled to get the ship's lifeboat on board. It had probably filled with water and was in danger of sinking. The passengers and crew were called upon to help raise the lifeboat out of the sea, and Luke's use of "we" (27:16) indicates that he and Paul and Aristarcus helped.

Finding it impossible to navigate, the captain decided to run before the storm. This decision was not without its danger. Neither sun nor stars had been seen for many days and so no one had any idea of where they were. They feared that they might be far to the south and run aground on the sandbars of Syrtis. This is a particularly dangerous part of the North African coast, and modern underwater archaeology has shown that these sandbars became the graveyard of many ships (27:17).

Those on board the galleon faced an even more prevalent danger. The ship was in danger of breaking up and so the crew lightened the vessel by jettisoning the cargo. When this proved insufficient, they also threw the ship's tackle overboard (27:18-19).

The days dragged on with the darkness of night being replaced by the monotonous gloom of a sunless day. By this time all on board had grown accustomed to their wet clothes hanging on their bodies like rags. Their discomfort was aggravated, however, by the strong wind that caused their tattered garments to cling to them, thus intensifying the cold. Depression settled like a wet blanket over those on the ship. Passengers and crew alike lost all hope of being saved. It was at this time that Paul stood up and said:

> "Men, you should have taken my advice not to sail from Crete; then you would have spared yourselves this damage and loss. But now I urge you to keep up your courage, because not one of you will be lost; only the ship will be destroyed. Last night an angel of the God whose I am and whom I serve stood beside me and said, 'Do not be afraid, Paul. You must stand trial before Caesar; and God has graciously given you the lives of all who sail with you.' So keep up your courage, men, for I have faith in God that it will happen just as he told me. Nevertheless, we must run aground on some island" (27:21-26).

Paul may have been a prisoner, but his leadership skills were evident on this occasion. It is not difficult to imagine the plight of all on board. Morale was at a low ebb. The cables undergirding the ship were being strained to the utmost. Waves were breaking over the sides, and it is no wonder men and crew felt that at any moment they might find themselves swept into the raging sea. They knew that in such stormy waters they would be unable to swim, and would sink into the darkness of the ocean's depths never to be seen or heard from again.

When the day was about to dawn, Paul was encouraging them all to take some food, saying, "Today is the fourteenth day that you have been constantly watching and going without eating, having taken nothing. Therefore I encourage you to take some food, for this is for your preservation, for not a hair from the head of any of you will perish." Having said this, he took bread and gave thanks to God in the presence of all, and he broke it and began to eat. All of them were encouraged and they themselves also took food. All of us in the ship were two hundred and seventy-six persons. When they had eaten enough, they began to lighten the ship by throwing the sacks of wheat into the sea (27:33-38).

Following Paul's encouraging words, and fortified by the food they had eaten, the spirits of passengers and crew revived.

That night, around midnight, some sailors surmised that they were approaching land. They may have heard the distant sound of waves breaking on rocks, or perhaps the ship was no longer pitching and rolling as formerly. Whatever the reason they took a sounding and found the depth of the sea to be only one hundred and twenty feet. A short time later they took another sounding and found the depth to be only ninety feet.

Malta, 27:39–28:10

When the day dawned they could dimly discern a bay, and determined to run the ship aground on the sandy beach. Their efforts, however, were frustrated because strong cross-currents had built up a sandbar. The bow of the ship stuck fast in the sand, leaving the stern exposed to the waves. It soon began to break up.

At this point the soldiers wanted to kill the prisoners, fearing that they might escape. It was an old custom that if a captor lost a captive, his life was forfeited. The centurion, however, stopped them from terminating those being taken to Rome for trial. Luke adds that he was motivated by a desire to spare Paul. Instead, he instructed all who could swim to jump overboard and swim to land, and those who could not swim were to follow on pieces of the ship (27:39-44a). "And so it happened that they all were brought safely to land" (27:44b).

James Smith has identified the bay where the shipwreck took place, and it is today called "St. Paul's Bay."[103] Because the island had been colonized by Phoenicians ten centuries before the birth of Christ, the local peasants spoke a Phoenician dialect that closely resembled Hebrew and Aramaic. This enabled Paul (and perhaps others) to converse with them, and they found out that they were now on the island of Malta.

---

103. Smith, *The Voyage and Shipwreck of St. Paul*, 141.

The Greeks called all foreigners who did not speak Greek *"barbaroi,"* "barbarians" (28:2, 4), and that was the name they applied to the Maltese people. The conduct of the peasants living on this island shows them to be the opposite of illiterate savages. Motivated by the plight of the passengers and crew so recently saved from drowning, they built a fire for them. This gave them some slender comfort from the rain and early morning wind.

Paul assisted in gathering "a large bundle of firewood." While he was placing these on the fire a viper, dislodged by the heat, slithered out of the fire and bit his hand.[104]

The islanders obviously recognized this snake to be poisonous, and watched to see if Paul's hand would swell or if he would fall down dead. They also concluded that *Dike*, their goddess of retributive justice, had caught up with Paul and was punishing him for past crimes. When Paul did not succumb to the effects of the venom these Maltese onlookers changed their minds and concluded that Paul must be a god (28:1-6).

Superstitious people oscillate from one viewpoint to another. Paul was not being punished for past sins, and neither was he a god. Though Satan may have been trying to kill Paul,[105] fearing the good he would do, the truth of the

---

104. Verse 3 uses *echnida*, the usual word for snake, whereas verse 4 describes the reptile as a *therion*, the general name among the Greek writers for serpents, vipers, and other noxious creatures.

matter lies in God's providence and sovereign protection of him.

Whether the incident on the beach had a bearing on what happened next, we do not know. Luke informs us that there was an estate near the beach belonging to a prominent citizen named Publius. He entertained Paul and his party in his home for three days. While in Publius' home Paul learned that his host's father was ill (28:8). Scholars have concluded that the "fever and dysentery" from which this elderly gentleman suffered was "Malta fever"–a common ailment along the Mediterranean coast. The fever comes from a micro-organism that is introduced into the body via the milk of Maltese goats

Paul healed the man instantly, and as news spread, people from all across the island brought their sick to Paul in order that they might be healed (28:9).

So grateful were the people that they gave gifts and supplies to all the castaways.

Arrival in Rome, 28:11-24

After three months Julius was able to secure passage for his crew and the prisoners on another Alexandrian ship that had wintered in one of the island's bays. Luke draws attention to the fact that its carved and painted figurehead was of the *Dioskouroi* (i.e., the twins Castor and Pollux). In Greek

---

105. He had tried to use mob violence in Jerusalem, assassins on the way from Jerusalem to Caesarea, storms at sea, and now a poisonous snake.

and Roman mythology these sons of Zeus/Jupiter were the gods of navigation and the patrons of seafarers.

Once aboard this ship they set out for Rome. The journey must have been an exciting one. Their first stop was Syracuse, the capital of Sicily (28:12). They stayed there for three days, possibly off loading or taking on new cargo. Then they put out to sea again, but this time the weather did not permit smooth sailing, for they had to make a circuit in order to reach Rhegium, a port on the toe of Italy. Luke's reference to "we circled around" possibly means that they had to tack back and forth.

After this they sailed through the Straits of Messina. Greek mythology created numerous stories about two terrible creatures, Scilla and Charybdis, who guarded the narrow passage between Italy and Sicily. These horrifying tales date back to the time of Odysseus and describe how three times a day Charybdis would gulp down the waters of the sea and then spew them out again. Ships passing by when one of these phenomena occurred were drawn under the water and only broken parts of the vessel were disgorged. And Scylla was also to be feared. She was portrayed as a beautiful women. The lower part of her body, however, was comprised of six vicious dogs who grasped and devoured seamen as they passed by.[106]

The ship made it safely to Puteoli on the Gulf of Naples. Paul now was nearing the end of his journey. He and the other prisoners disembarked at Puteoli, and there Paul found some believers who had traveled from the Forum of Appius and the Three Taverns to meet him. It must have been an emotional moment for Paul and his party to meet with these Christians. They then escorted him to Rome.

On his arrival in Rome Paul was accorded *custodia militaris* which permitted him to live in his own lodgings, while being chained to a soldier who belonged to the Praetorian Guard (28:16). The guard was changed periodically, and this gave Paul new opportunities for evangelism. Many of those to whom Paul was chained came to faith in Christ (see Philippians 1:12-13).

Three days after his arrival in Rome Paul called together the leaders of the Jews. When they all were assembled, he said:

"Men and brethren, though I have done nothing against our people or the customs of our fathers, yet I was delivered as a prisoner from Jerusalem into the hands of the Romans, who, when they had examined me, wanted to let me go, because there was no cause for putting me to death. But when the Jews spoke against it, I was compelled to appeal to Caesar, not that I had anything of

---

106. Avery, ed., Greek Mythology and Legend, 140, 484-85. See also Homer's Odyssey (XII:223-74 and XII:429-53). Homer describes how fearful the Straits of Messina were to ancient mariners. Ernle Bradford, an Oxford scholar who for more than twenty years sailed the Mediterranean, wrote a book entitled *Ulysses Found*. He records how volcanic eruptions that were common in the area changed the geography of the sea floor so that the phenomena that frightened Odysseus/Ulysses no longer instilled fear in the hearts of travelers in the 1st Century B.C./A.D.

which to accuse my nation. For this reason therefore I have called for you, to see you and speak with you, because for the hope of Israel I am bound with this chain."

Then they said to him, "We neither received letters from Judea concerning you, nor have any of the brethren who came reported or spoken any evil of you. But we desire to hear from you what you think; for concerning this sect, we know that it is spoken against everywhere."

So when they had appointed him a day, many came to him at his lodging. There, from morning till evening, he explained and solemnly testified of the kingdom of God, persuading them concerning Jesus from both the Law of Moses and the Prophets (28:17-23).

We are not surprised that no communique had come to Rome from Jerusalem, for the religious leaders had no legitimate grounds upon which to condemn Paul. They were content that he was under a cloud of suspicion and confined so that he could not go about preaching about the Gospel.

The Jewish leaders wanted to hear more of his views, and so listened to his lengthy discourse. Some were convinced that Jesus was the Messiah, but others were not, and inasmuch as they disagreed among themselves they began to leave. Seeing this, Paul made a final statement:

"Well spake the Holy Spirit through Isaiah the prophet unto your fathers, saying, 'Go to this people, and say, "By hearing you shall hear, and shall in no wise understand; and seeing you shall see, and shall in no wise perceive", for this people's heart is waxed gross, and their ears are dull of hearing, and their eyes they have closed; lest, hapily they should perceive with their eyes, and hear with their ears, and understand with their heart, and should turn again, and I should heal them' " (28:25-27).

Because of the Jews' deliberate rejection of the gospel, Paul wanted them to know that God's salvation was being offered to Gentiles. Then he added, "They (the Gentiles) will listen with open ears" and be saved (28:28).

During Paul's two year incarceration in Rome he welcomed all who came to him (Jews and Gentiles). Among these who sought out the apostle was Onesimus (Philemon 1:10-16), Epaphras (Colossians 1:7; 4:12) and Epaphroditus (Philippians 1:18).

Luke concludes his treatise by saying, "Paul stayed two full years in his own rented quarters and ... preached the kingdom of God and taught concerning the Lord Jesus Christ with all openness, unhindered" (28:30-31). After that, because no formal charge had been brought to Nero, he was released.

But didn't Paul suffer martyrdom in Rome? Yes he did. In point of fact he suffered two Roman imprisonments.

Bible critics are opposed to two imprisonments, even though the early Church Fathers from Clement of Rome to Eusebius favored such a view. The question arises, Do we have any biblical proof of Paul's release and subsequent ministry before being rearrested and taken back to Rome? It has been pointed out that Paul was compelled to leave Trophimus sick in Miletus (2 Timothy 4:20). This could not have occurred on Paul's last visit to Jerusalem, for Trophimus was not left behind (cf. Acts 20:4; 21:29). To make this incident possible there must have been a release from the first imprisonment and an interval of ministry (perhaps even to Spain) before being was rearrested, imprisoned, tried, and executed.

CHAPTER TWELVE

PAUL'S SUCCESSOR

While writing this chapter on Timothy I was reminded of Christmas gifts my wife would give our grandsons when they were young. With wisdom far beyond my own she would select jigsaw puzzles for them. My expectation was that they would play with the box and leave the pieces of the puzzle alone. To my surprise the other gifts my grandsons received remained unopened and each one would eagerly clear a table or place on the carpet and begin to piece together the fragments that made up the whole.

Studying the life of Timothy is similar to the task to which my grandsons set themselves. It requires gathering together all the references to Timothy's life, arranging them in order, and deducing from them the contribution of his life to the progress of the church.

Timothy became Paul's successor, and the way in which Paul instructed his young protégé serves as a blueprint for ministry today. We have a brief summary of his approach in 2 Timothy 2:1-2, *"You therefore, my son, be strong in the grace that is in Christ Jesus. The things which you have heard from me in the presence of many witnesses, entrust these to faithful men who will be able to teach others also."*

Paul had many friends. Many of them labored for the Lord and some even started house churches. Paul's relationship with Timothy, however, was different. He groomed

Timothy to be his successor. Timothy was not an apostle in the same way Paul was, but he was a minister of the gospel to people in Asia Minor (modern Turkey) and Europe. Some evidence of the close friendship Paul had with Timothy can be gleaned from the fact that he always spoke of him in terms of the utmost praise, and joined Timothy's name with his own in six of his letters. Timothy seems to have been of like mind with Paul (cf. 1 Corinthians 4:17; 16:10-11; Philippians 2:19-23), and time and again Paul spoke of him as his "son" (1 Timothy 1:18; 2 Timothy 1:2; 2:1).

Timothy's Early Life

Timothy was evidently from Lystra. His mother was a Jewish believer, but his father was a Greek[107] (16:1). From an early age Timothy had been taught the Scriptures by his mother, Eunice, and his grandmother, Lois (cf. 2 Timothy 3:12-17). Just when Timothy accepted Christ as his Savior is not told us. It may have been on Paul's first missionary journey (c. A.D. 46-48) when Paul and Barnabas visited the southern portion of Galatia (14:1). It was in Lystra that Paul was stoned, and this must have had a profound effect on young Timothy (14:8-20; cf. 2 Timothy 2:3; 3:10-11). Some writers believe that when Paul came back to life he was taken into Timothy's home and cared for by Eunice and Lois.

---

107. Luke uses the imperfect *hyperchen*, "was," when speaking of Timothy's father. This has led some scholars to conclude that Timothy's father was dead.

On the second journey (c. A.D. 49-52) Paul and Silas revisited this area and strengthened the churches. While in the region of Derbe and Lystra the leadership of these churches recommended Timothy to the missionaries (16:2). Paul wanted to have Timothy accompany them, and take the place of John Mark. Because he had not been circumcised at birth we may presume that his father had in all likelihood objected to the practice his wife's religion. Now, however, because his father probably was dead Paul took Timothy and circumcised him (16:3). After this he was formally set apart as an evangelist by the laying on of hands (1 Timothy 4:14; 2 Timothy 4:5). Because it was Paul's policy to minister first in the synagogues of the cities through which they passed, Timothy would be of most help in the furtherance of the gospel as a Jew (cf. 1 Corinthians 9:20-23).

Timothy's Early Ministry

From this time on Timothy was one of Paul's most constant companions. He, together with Silas and Luke, journeyed to Philippi (16:12), and on the way the Apostle probably finely honed his doctrinal beliefs by building on the instruction his young assistant had received from his mother and grandmother. Lessons in guidance were added to the "curriculum" when the Holy Spirit forbade them to preach in Asia and closed the door to ministry in Bithynia. Finally they came to Troas, and that was where Paul had his vision of a man from Macedonia pleading with him to come over into Europe and help them.

A profitable ministry in Philippi ensued, but before long the missionaries were falsely accused, flogged, and thrown into jail. Though Timothy was not imprisoned with Paul and Silas his filial devotion was real (Philippians 2:19-22). Paul's confidence in him was such that, after leaving the city and journeying on to Thessalonica, he sent Timothy back to Philippi to watch over the infant church.

Trouble followed the missionaries and after they had ministered in Berea (from whence Paul was compelled to flee to Athens), Paul left Timothy and Silas behind to further establish the believers in the faith (17:14). From these experiences Timothy began to realize something of the cost involved in being a disciple of Christ.

Later on Timothy joined Paul in Athens (17:15), but he was soon sent back to Thessalonica to further establish the Christians there who were enduring persecution (1 Thessalonians 3:1-2).

After a disappointing ministry in Athens Paul moved on to Corinth. Timothy and Silas joined him there, but before long Timothy was sent back to Thessalonica (18:5*a*; 1 Thessalonians 3:2). He possessed special gifts for comforting and encouraging believers, and so winsome was his ministry in that city that when Paul wrote his first and second letters to the believers there he joined Timothy's name with his own (cf. 1 Thessalonians 1:1; 2 Thessalonians 1:1).

Timothy's Later Ministry

Of the following five years of Timothy's life we have no record. We do know that the Apostle Paul ministered in Ephesus (19:8-22), and we have no doubt that during all this time Timothy was faithful in discharging whatever duties the Apostle Paul assigned him. These probably included being sent to minister in Colossae (Colossians 1:1; Philemon 1:1).

From Ephesus Paul sent Timothy to Corinth to handle some difficult matters (1 Corinthians 4;17). He intended his letter to the Corinthians to arrive before Timothy's visit, but apparently there was a delay and the mail did not reach Corinth in time. His commendation of Timothy did not secure for Timothy a warm reception. Paul feared that some haughty and puffed up individuals might belittle Timothy on account of his youth, disregard what he had to say, and intimidate his young protégé (cf. 1 Corinthians 16:10-11).

It would appear as if Timothy's ministry in Corinth was a failure. We are not told how he returned to Paul, only that he was with the Apostle when he wrote to the Corinthians from Macedonia (20:2-4). It is significant that Paul did not blame Timothy for what happened in Corinth. Instead he encouraged him by referring to him as my "workfellow" (Roman 16:21). And when the Apostle revisited Corinth, Timothy was with him.

Timothy also earned the respect of leaders in different churches, for in 20:4 he was one of those chosen to take the contribution of the churches to the poor in Jerusalem. Paul went as well, but as we know, he was imprisoned first in Caesarea and then in Rome.

Timothy's Ministry During Paul's Imprisonment

From Philippians 1:1 we know that Timothy was in Rome with Paul. Of particular importance is the Apostle's tribute to Timothy in Philippians 2:19-23, where he describes Timothy as a man who was free from all self-seeking and devoted to the care of the churches. This praise led Herbert Seekings to remark, "Never did Paul allow himself such freedom in the praise of his co-workers as in this tender outburst of feeling concerning one who had toiled with him in the holy work and whom he had come to esteem as a genuine son."[108]

Timothy was also with Paul in Rome when the epistles to the Philippians, and Philemon were written (cf. Philippians 1:1; 2:19; Colossians 1:1 and Philemon 1:1).

Timothy's Ministry After Paul's Release

It follows from 1 Timothy 1:3 that after Paul's release from his imprisonment Timothy and Paul revisited proconsular Asia. The Apostle then continued his journey to Macedonia while Timothy remained, reluctantly, at Ephesus (2 Timothy 1:4) to check if possible the growth of heresy and licentiousness that had sprung up in that area.

Timothy's task was a difficult one. As Paul's representative he had to exercise rule over the elders, some of whom were older than himself (1 Timothy 4:12); render judgments (1 Timothy 5:1,19-20); regulate the almsgiving to widows

---

108. Seekings, *Men of the Pauline Circle*, 60.

in the church (1 Timothy 5:3-10); and ordain elders and deacons. These duties, together with the danger of being entangled in the disputes of rival sects, made Paul anxious for the steadfastness of his disciple.

Paul, as we have noted, had been released from confinement in Rome, but after a period of public ministry was rearrested, tried, and sentenced to death. Among the last recorded words Paul addressed to Timothy were his desire to see him again. He also asked Timothy to *come before winter* (2 Timothy 4:9, 13, 21a).[109] Whether Timothy reached the aged apostle before his execution has not been told us.

THE EMERGING PICTURE

As we look back over Timothy's life and ministry and piece together the information that has been given to us we find that Timothy must have been a devoted friend, warm-hearted and affectionate, committed to his spiritual father, and happy to work alongside the great apostle. He lacked Paul's bold assertiveness, and was evidently inclined to be introspective. And perhaps he suffered from a certain insecurity (note 109, Timothy 4:12). Seen as a whole, Timothy stands out as an excellent servant of Christ, and one from whom we have much to learn.

---

109. W. M. Ramsay, *Pictures of the Apostolic Church* (Grand Rapids: Baker, 1959), 332-37, and 338-43.

www.ingramcontent.com/pod-product-compliance
Lightning Source LLC
Chambersburg PA
CBHW071437160426
43195CB00013B/1937